UNDERSTANDING AND USING

English Grammar

FOURTH EDITION

WORKBOOK

Volume B

PEARSON
Longman

Betty S. Azar
Rachel Spack Koch
Stacy A. Hagen

Understanding and Using English Grammar, Fourth Edition
Workbook, Volume B

Pearson Education, 10 Bank Street, White Plains, NY 10606

Staff credits: The people who made up the ***Understanding and Using
English Grammar, Fourth Edition, Workbook Volume B*** team, representing
editorial, production, design, and manufacturing, are Dave Dickey, Christine
Edmonds, Ann France, Margo Grant, Amy McCormick, and Robert Ruvo.

Text composition: S4Carlisle Publishing Services
Text font: 10.5/12 Plantin

Illustrations: Don Martinetti—pages 160, 162 (bottom), 195, A15, A23;
  Chris Pavely—pages 123, 140, 142, 143, 151, 155, 158, 159, 162 (top),
  163, 165, 174, 180, 198, 203

ISBN 10: 0-13-241545-3
ISBN 13: 978-0-13-241545-3

Printed in the United States of America
4 5 6 7 8 9 10—V016—14 13 12

Contents

Chapter 17   ADVERB CLAUSES

Chapter 18   REDUCTION OF ADVERB CLAUSES TO MODIFYING ADVERBIAL PHRASES

Chapter 19   CONNECTIVES THAT EXPRESS CAUSE AND EFFECT, CONTRAST, AND CONDITION

Special Workbook Section   PHRASAL VERBS

Preface

The *Understanding and Using English Grammar Workbook* is a place for students to explore and practice English grammar on their own. It is a place where they can test and fine-tune their understandings of English structures and improve their abilities to use English meaningfully and correctly. All of the exercises have been designed for independent study, but this book is also a resource for teachers who need exercise material for additional classwork, homework, testing, or individualized instruction.

The *Workbook* is keyed to the explanatory grammar charts found in *Understanding and Using English Grammar, Fourth Edition*, a classroom teaching text for students of English as a second or foreign language, as well as in the accompanying *Chartbook*, a reference grammar with no exercises.

The answers to the practices can be found in the *Answer Key* in the back of the *Workbook*. Its pages are perforated so that they can be detached to make a separate booklet. However, if teachers want to use the *Workbook* as a classroom teaching text, the *Answer Key* can be removed at the beginning of the term.

A special *Workbook* section called *Phrasal Verbs*, not available in the main text, is included in the *Appendix*. This section provides a reference list of common phrasal verbs along with a variety of exercises for independent practice.

Chapter 12
Noun Clauses

▶ **Practice 1. Introduction.** (Chart 12-1)

<u>Underline</u> the noun clauses. Some sentences don't have one.

1. I couldn't hear what he said.
2. What did he say?
3. I don't know what happened.
4. Why are you calling me?
5. I wonder why Dora is calling me.
6. Do you know who that man is?
7. Do you know where Hank lives?
8. What are they doing?
9. What they are doing is wrong.
10. What should I say?
11. I don't know what I should say.
12. Where will she live?

▶ **Practice 2. Questions and noun clauses beginning with a question word.**
(Chart 12-2)

Complete the sentences with the given words.

1. they \ do \ want

   What _____?

2. want \ they \ what

   I don't know _____.

3. Stacy \ live \ does

   Where _____?

4. lives \ where \ Stacy

   Can you tell me _____?

5. what \ Carl \ likes

   Do you know _____?

6. Carl \ does \ like

   What _____?

7. is \ Lina \ going

   Where _____?

8. is \ where \ going \ Lina

   I wonder _____.

► **Practice 3. Questions and noun clauses beginning with a question word.**
   (Chart 12-2)

Add punctuation and capitalization. Underline the noun clause if there is one.

1. Where does Lee live does he live downtown

   Where does Lee live? **D**oes he live downtown?

2. I don't know where he lives

   I don't know <u>where he lives</u>.

3. What does Sandra want do you know

4. Do you know what Sandra wants

5. What Yoko knows is important to us

6. We talked about what Yoko knows

7. What do you think did you tell your professor what you think

8. My professor knows what I think

9. Where is the bus stop do you know where the bus stop is

10. What did he report what he reported is important

► **Practice 4. Noun clauses beginning with a question word.** (Chart 12-2)
Change each question in parentheses to a noun clause.

1. (*How far is it?*) I don't know _____ *how far it is* _____.

2. (*What is that on the table?*) I don't know _____.

3. (*How much did it cost?*) Ask her _____.

4. (*What did he say?*) _____ is very interesting.

5. (*When are they leaving?*) Do you know _____?

6. (*Which road should we take?*) Can you tell us _____?

7. (*Who called?*) Please tell me _____.

8. (*What's happening?*) Do you know _____?

9. (*Why do they work at night?*) Nobody knows _____.

10. (*What are they trying to do?*) _____ is difficult.

11. (*What kind of insects are these?*) I don't know _____.

12. (*Whose keys are these?*) I wonder _____.

► **Practice 5. Questions and noun clauses beginning with a question word.**
   (Charts 12-1 and 12-2; Appendix Charts B-1 and B-2)

Make a question from the given sentence. The words in parentheses should be the answer to the question you make. Use a question word (**who, what, how,** etc.). Then change the question to a noun clause.

1. That man is (*Mr. Robertson*).

   QUESTION: _____ *Who is that man?* _____

   NOUN CLAUSE: I want to know _____ *who that man is.* _____

2. George lives (*in Los Angeles*).

   QUESTION: _____

   NOUN CLAUSE: I want to know _____

3. Ann bought (*a new dictionary*).

   QUESTION: _____

   NOUN CLAUSE: Do you know _____

4. It is (*350 miles*) to Denver from here.

   QUESTION: _____

   NOUN CLAUSE: I need to know _____

5. Jack was late for class (*because he missed the bus*).

   QUESTION: _____

   NOUN CLAUSE: The teacher wants to know _____

6. That is (*Ann's*) pen.

   QUESTION: _____

   NOUN CLAUSE: Tom wants to know _____

7. Alex saw (*Ms. Frost*) at the meeting.

   QUESTION: _____

   NOUN CLAUSE: I don't know _____

8. (*Jack*) saw Ms. Frost at the meeting.

   QUESTION: _____

   NOUN CLAUSE: Do you know _____

9. Alice likes (*this*) book best, (*not that one*).

   QUESTION: _____

   NOUN CLAUSE: I want to know _____

10. The plane is supposed to land (*at 7:14 P.M.*).

    QUESTION: _____

    NOUN CLAUSE: Could you tell me _____

▶ **Practice 6. Noun clauses beginning with a question word.** (Chart 12-2)
Write the letter of the phrase in the list to complete each conversation.

   a. what did he say
   b. what he said
   c. where are you going
   d. where you are going

   e. which bus should we take to the stadium
   f. which bus we should take to the stadium
   g. why did she do that
   h. why she did that

1. A: What did the professor just say?

   B: I don't know _____. I couldn't understand anything.

2. A: Hey, Kim, _____?

   B: Downtown. We're going to the new show at the art museum.

3. A: Hello, there! You look lost. Can I help you?

   B: Yes, _____? We want to go to the football stadium in Fairfield.

4. A: Turn the TV up, please. I can't hear the weather reporter. Linda, _____ ?

   B: He said that there will be a lot of rain tomorrow.

5. A: Hello! Can you please tell us _____?

   B: Sorry, I don't know. I'm a stranger here myself.

6. A: I told you that we are going to Bermuda for a vacation, didn't I?

   B: Well, you told us about the vacation, but you didn't say _____.

7. A: Ms. Holsum just quit her job at the university.

   B: Oh, _____? That was such a good job!

   A: Nobody knows _____. It's a mystery.

▶ **Practice 7. Noun clauses beginning with *whether* or *if*.** (Chart 12-3)
Circle the letters of all the correct completions for each sentence.

1. We don't know _____.
   a. whether it will snow
   b. whether or not it will snow
   c. whether it will snow or not

   d. if it will snow
   e. if or not it will snow
   f. if it will snow or not

2. _____ doesn't matter to me.
   a. Whether or not it snows
   b. Whether it snows or not
   c. Whether does it snow or not

   d. If or not it snows
   e. If snows or not
   f. If does it snow

3. I wonder _____.
   a. whether or not does she know
   b. whether she knows or not
   c. whether does she know

   d. if does she know
   e. if she knows or not
   f. if or not she does know

▶ **Practice 8. Review.** (Charts 12-2 and 12-3)
Complete the questions using *Do you know*.

Do you know . . .

1. How much does this book cost? _____

2. When is Flight 62 expected? _____

3. Where is the nearest phone? _____

4. Is this word spelled correctly? _____

5. What time is it? _____

6. Is this information correct? _____

7. How much does it cost to fly from Toronto to London? _____

8. Where is the bus station? _____

9. Whose pen is this? _____

10. Does this bus go downtown? _____

▶ **Practice 9. Question words followed by infinitives.** (Chart 12-4)
Complete the sentences in Column A with a phrase from Column B.

Column A

1. Where can I find fresh fish?
   I don't know __g__ .
2. Which person will be a better president?
   I don't know ____ .
3. Who can I get to repair the TV?
   I don't know ____ .
4. Should I get another job?
   I don't know ____ .
5. What's good to eat here?
   I don't know ____ .
6. How far is the airport from here?
   I don't know ____ .
7. What should it cost?
   I don't know ____ .
8. Do we need a lot of sandwiches for the party?
   I don't know ____ .

Column B

a. who to vote for
b. how far the airport is from here
c. whether to look for one
d. how much to spend
e. how to fix it
f. what to order
✓g. where to buy it
h. how many to prepare

▶ **Practice 10. Noun clauses beginning with *that*.** (Chart 12-5)
Complete the sentences. Choose a word from the list. More than one word may be appropriate.

angry	confident	lucky	relieved
aware	disappointed	proud	worried

1. We are _____ that our son graduated first in his class. We are not
   surprised — he is an excellent student.

2. I am _____ that the store owner cheated me. That was awful!

3. Our teacher is _____ that all the students did poorly on the test.
   However, she is encouraging them to do well on the next test.

4. I was not _____ that our boss hired a new assistant. When did this
   happen?

5. It was _____ that we got off the elevator when we did. Just after we got
   off, it got stuck between floors, and the other passengers were inside for three hours!

6. Lee always wins the Ping-Pong tournaments at our community center. He is
   _____ that he will win the one next weekend.

7. We were very _____ that the hurricane was coming our way. But it
   changed course and went out to sea instead. Now we are _____ that the
   hurricane didn't hit us.

► **Practice 11. Noun clauses beginning with *that*.** (Chart 12-5)
Rewrite the sentences in *italics* in two ways. Use the words from the original sentence.

1. *Nobody stopped to help Sam on the road. That is surprising.*

    a. It _____is surprising that_____ nobody stopped to help Sam on the road.

    b. The fact that _____nobody stopped to help Sam_____ on the road

       _____is surprising_____ .

2. *People in modern cities are distrustful of each other. That is unfortunate.*

    a. It _____ people in modern cities are distrustful of each other.

    b. That _____

       distrustful of each other _____ .

3. *People in my village always help each other. That is still true.*

    a. It _____

       in my village always help each other.

    b. That _____ always

       _____ each other _____ .

4. *People need each other and need to help each other. That is undeniably true.*

    a. It _____ people need each other and need to help each other.

    b. That _____ and need to help each other

       _____ .

5. *People in cities live in densely populated areas but don't know their neighbors. That seems strange to me.*

    a. It _____ me _____ in

       densely populated areas but don't know their neighbors.

    b. The fact that _____ live in densely populated areas but

       _____ seems strange to me.

► **Practice 12. Quoted speech.** (Chart 12-6)
Add punctuation and capitalization.

1. Millie said   there's an important meeting at three o'clock today

2. There's an important meeting at three o'clock today   she said

3. There is   said Millie   an important meeting at three o'clock today

4. There is an important meeting today   it's about the new rules   said Millie

5. Where is the meeting   Carl asked

6. Robert replied   it's in the conference room

7. How long will it last   asked Ali

8. I don't know how long it will last   replied Millie

9. I'll be a little late   said Robert   I have another meeting until 3:00 P.M. today

10. Who is speaking at the meeting   asked Robert

11. I am not sure who is speaking   said Millie   but you'd better be there   everybody is supposed

to be there

▶ **Practice 13. Quoted speech.** (Chart 12-6)
Read this familiar story about the rabbit and the turtle. Punctuate the quoted speech in the numbered sections.

One day a rabbit laughed at a turtle because the turtle was very slow.

(1) You are so slow Mr turtle   said the rabbit   and I am

very fast.

(2) I don't know about that   said the turtle   let's have a

race   we will run for five miles and see who wins

(3) I agree   said the rabbit

They started off, and the rabbit was so far ahead that he laughed and laughed. He said to himself:

(4) I am so far ahead of the turtle   I am going to take a little nap right here   it is going to

take a long time before that turtle can catch up with me

And so, while the rabbit was taking his nap, the turtle came along slowly but steadily. The turtle passed by the sleeping rabbit and won the race.

(5) The turtle looked back at the rabbit and exclaimed   slow but steady wins the race   who's

laughing now mr rabbit

▶ **Practice 14. Reported speech.** (Chart 12-7)
Complete the sentences with the correct form of the verb.

1. Tom said, "I am busy."   Tom said that he _____was_____ busy.
2. Tom said, "I need some help."   Tom said that he _____ some help.
3. Tom said, "I am having a good time."   Tom said that he _____ a good time.
4. Tom said, "I have finished my work."   Tom said that he _____ his work.
5. Tom said, "I finished it."   Tom said that he _____ it.
6. Tom said, "I will arrive at noon."   Tom said that he _____ at noon.
7. Tom said, "I am going to be there."   Tom said that he _____ there.

8. Tom said, "I can solve that problem." Tom said that he _____ that problem.

9. Tom said, "I may come early." Tom said that he _____ early.

10. Tom said, "I might come early." Tom said that he _____ early.

11. Tom said, "I must leave at eight." Tom said that he _____ at eight.

12. Tom said, "I have to leave at eight." Tom said that he _____ at eight.

13. Tom said, "I should go to the library." Tom said that he _____ to the library.

14. Tom said, "Stay here." Tom told me _____ here.

▶ **Practice 15. Reported speech.** (Chart 12-7)
Complete the sentences by changing the quoted speech to reported speech. Use formal sequence of tenses as appropriate. Pay attention to whether the reporting verb is past or present.

1. I asked Martha, "Are you planning to enter law school?"

   I asked Martha _____*if / whether she was planning*_____ to enter law school.

2. Ed just asked me, "What time does the movie begin?"

   Ed wants to know _____.

3. Fred asked, "Can we still get tickets for the concert?"

   Fred asked _____ tickets for the concert.

4. Thomas said to us, "How can I help you?"

   Thomas wants to know _____ us.

5. Eva asked, "Can you help me, Mario?"

   Eva asked Mario _____ her.

6. Charles said, "When will the final decision be made?"

   Charles wanted to know _____.

7. Frank asked Carla, "Where have you been all afternoon?"

   Frank asked Carla _____ all afternoon.

8. Jaime just asked, "What is Kim's native language?"

   Jaime wants to know _____.

9. I asked myself, "Am I doing the right thing?"

   I wondered _____ the right thing.

10. George asked me, "What time do I have to be at the lab in the morning?"

    George asked me _____ to be at the lab in the morning.

11. Yuki asked, "Who should I give this message to?"

    Yuki asked me _____ to.

12. Nancy asked, "Why didn't you call me?"

    Nancy wanted to know _____ her.

▶ Practice 16. Reported speech. (Chart 12-7)

Complete the sentences using the information in the conversation. Use past verb forms in the noun clauses if appropriate and possible.

Conversation 1.

"Where are you going, Ann?" I asked.

"I'm on my way to the market," she replied. "Do you want to come with me?"

"I'd like to, but I have to stay home. I have a lot of work to do."

"OK," Ann said. "Is there anything I can pick up for you at the market?"

"How about a few bananas? And some apples if they're fresh?"

"Sure. I'd be happy to."

When I asked Ann where she _____ , she said she _____
                                          1   2
on her way to the market and _____ me to come with her. I said I
                                              3
_____ to, but that I _____ to stay home because I
              4   5
_____ a lot of work to do. Ann kindly asked me if there _____ anything she
        6   7
_____ pick up for me at the market. I asked her to pick up a few bananas and some
        8
apples if they _____ fresh. She said she'd be happy to.
                          9

Conversation 2.

"Where are you from?" asked the passenger sitting next to me on the plane.

"Chicago," I said.

"That's nice. I'm from Mapleton. It's a small town in northern Michigan. Have you heard of it?"

"Oh yes, I have," I said. "Michigan is a beautiful state. I've been there on vacation many times."

"Were you in Michigan on vacation this year?"

"No. I went far away from home this year. I went to India," I replied.

"Oh, that's nice. Is it a long drive from Chicago to India?" she asked me. My mouth fell open.
I didn't know how to respond. Some people certainly need to study geography.

The passenger sitting next to me on the plane _____ me where I _____
                                                              1   2
from. I _____ her I _____ from Chicago. She _____ that she
            3   4   5
_____ from Mapleton, a small town in northern Michigan. She wondered if I
        6
_____ of it, and I told her that I _____ . I went on to say that I
              7   8
thought Michigan _____ a beautiful state and explained that I _____
                            9   10
there on vacation many times. She _____ me if I _____ in
                                              11   12
Michigan on vacation this year. I replied that I _____ and _____ her that I
                                                          13   14
_____ far away, to India. Then she asked me if it _____ a long drive
              15   16
from Chicago to India! My mouth fell open. I didn't know how to respond. Some people certainly

need to study geography.

► **Practice 17. Using -ever words.** (Chart 12-8)
Complete each sentence with the correct **-ever** word.

1. As vice-president of international sales, Robert has complete control over his travel schedule.
   He can travel _____*whenever*_____ he wants.

2. Robert is free to decide which countries he will visit during his overseas trips. He can travel
   _____ he wants.

3. The English professor told us that we could write our papers on _____ subject
   we wanted as long as it related to the topics we discussed in class this semester.

4. I understand that the planes aren't flying because of the weather, but you have to come
   anyway. Get here _____ you can: take the train, take a bus, or drive. Just get
   here fast.

5. There are several appointment times available. You may select _____ one you
   prefer.

6. Linda is very amiable and gregarious. She makes friends with _____ she meets.

7. It doesn't matter what class you take to fulfill this requirement. Just take _____
   one fits best into your schedule.

8. _____ is the last to leave the room should turn off the lights and lock the door.

9. I know that Norman will succeed. He'll do _____ is required to succeed.

10. My wife and I are going to ride our bicycles across the country. We will ride for six to seven
    hours a day, and then we'll stop _____ we happen to be at the end of the day.

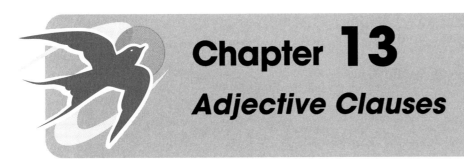

Chapter 13
Adjective Clauses

▶ **Practice 1. Adjective clause pronouns used as the subject.** (Chart 13-1)
Underline the adjective clause in each sentence. Draw an arrow to the word it modifies.

1. We are looking for a person who fixes computers.

2. I know a man who lives on a boat.

3. In our office, there is a woman who speaks four languages.

4. There are several people who are bilingual in the office.

5. I work in an office that is in an old building.

6. The building which we work in was built in 1890.

7. Two trees that were over two hundred years old were struck by lightning last night.

8. Two other trees which were nearby were not harmed.

9. The traffic jam was caused by one truck that had broken down.

10. The truck which caused the problem was in the middle of the highway.

▶ **Practice 2. Adjective clause pronouns used as the subject.** (Chart 13-1)
Circle the letter of all the possible completions for each sentence. Do not add any commas or capital letters.

1. I thanked the woman _____ brought back our lost cat.
   a. who   b. that   c. which   d. she

2. The aquarium is looking for new employees _____ know a lot about dolphins.
   a. who   b. that   c. which   d. they

3. What is the TV channel _____ has stories about animals?
   a. who   b. it   c. which   d. that

4. On my flight, there was a weight-lifter _____ didn't fit into the airplane seat.
   a. who   b. that   c. he   d. which

5. None of the houses _____ have protective shutters were damaged in the typhoon.
   a. who   b. that   c. which   d. they

6. I'm transferring to a school _____ has a well-known program in cinematography.
   a. who   b. that   c. which   d. it

► **Practice 3. Adjective clause pronouns as the object of a verb.** (Chart 13-2)
<u>Underline</u> the adjective clause in each sentence. Draw an arrow to the word it modifies.

1. There's the man that I met last night.

2. There's the woman that Sandro is going to marry.

3. All the people whom we invited have accepted the invitation.

4. The book which I just read is going to be made into a movie.

5. I can't figure out how to use the software program that Jason installed.

6. We are still living in the house we built in 1987.

7. What happened to the cake I left on the table?

8. I bought the book my professor wrote.

► **Practice 4. Adjective clause pronouns as the object of a verb.** (Chart 13-2)
Circle the letter of all the possible completions for each sentence.

1. That's the woman _____ the people elected.
   a. who   b. whom   c. that   d. which   e. she   f. Ø

2. The man _____ the police arrested was not the thief.
   a. whom   b. he   c. that   d. which   e. who   f. Ø

3. I'd already seen the movie _____ we rented last night
   a. who   b. it   c. Ø   d. which   e. that   f. whom

4. Ms. McCarthy is a teacher _____ everyone loves.
   a. who   b. whom   c. Ø   d. which   e. that   f. her

5. Many of the people _____ we met on our vacation were very friendly.
   a. who   b. which   c. that   d. whom   e. Ø   f. they

6. A man _____ I know is going to be interviewed on a morning TV program.
   a. who   b. that   c. whom   d. which   e. him   f. Ø

► **Practice 5. Adjective clause pronouns used as the subject or object of the verb.** (Charts 13-1 and 13-2)
Complete the sentences with the correct adjective clause.

1. The book was good. I read it.

   The book that ___I read was good___.

2. The movie was very sad. I saw it.

   The movie that _____.

3. Elephants are animals. They can live a long time.

   Elephants are animals that _____.

4. At the zoo, there were two fifty-year-old elephants. We photographed them.

   At the zoo, there were two fifty-year-old elephants which _____.

5. Sarah is a person. She does many things at the same time.

Sarah is a person who _____.

6. Bill is a person. You can trust him.

Bill is a person you _____.

7. The painting was valuable. The thieves stole it.

The painting _____.

▶ **Practice 6. Adjective clause pronouns used as the object of a preposition.**
    (Chart 13-3)

Circle the letter of all possible completions.

1. The person _____ was Bob Jones in the customer service department.

   a. which I spoke to   f. to who I spoke
   b. to which I spoke   g. that I spoke to
   c. whom I spoke to   h. to that I spoke
   d. to whom I spoke   i. I spoke to
   e. who I spoke to him   j. I spoke to him

2. This is the explanation _____.

   a. which I was referring to   f. that I was referring to
   b. to which I was referring   g. to that I was referring
   c. whom I was referring to   h. I was referring to
   d. to whom I was referring   i. I was referring to it
   e. which I was referring to it

▶ **Practice 7. Adjective clauses.** (Charts 13-1 → 13-3)
    Write all the possible completions for each sentence.

1. Mr. Green is the man [ ] I was talking about.

2. She is the woman [ ] sits next to me in class.

3. The hat [ ] Tom is wearing is unusual.

4. Hunger and poverty are worldwide problems to [ ] solutions must be found.

5. I enjoyed talking with the man [ ] I sat next to on the plane.

6. People [ ] fear flying avoid traveling by plane.

7. The people about [ ] the novelist wrote were factory workers and their families.

8. A barrel is a large container [ ] is made of wood or metal.

▶ **Practice 8. Adjective clauses.** (Charts 13-1 → 13-3)
Correct the errors in the adjective clauses. Do not change any punctuation.

1. That's a subject I don't want to talk about it.

2. A person who he writes with his left hand is called a lefty.

3. Our family brought home a new kitten that we found it at the animal shelter.

4. What is the name of the radio program to that many people listen on Saturday nights?

5. The candidate for who you vote should be honest.

6. Here's a picture of Nancy who I took with my cell phone.

7. People have high cholesterol should watch their diets.

8. Suzie is going to marry the man she has always loved him.

9. There's an article in today's newspaper about a woman that she is 7 feet tall.

10. Passengers which have children may board the plane first.

▶ **Practice 9. Whose vs. Who's.** (Chart 13-4)
Complete the sentences. Write the letter of the correct pronoun.

1. This class is for students _____ English needs improvement.
   a. who's   b. whose

2. Belinda is a student _____ good in both math and languages.
   a. who's   b. whose

3. Will the student _____ cell phone is ringing please turn it off?
   a. who's   b. whose

4. A customer _____ dissatisfied is not good for a business.
   a. who's   b. whose

5. The customer _____ young son was crying tried to comfort him.
   a. who's   b. whose

6. Life is sometimes difficult for a child _____ parents are divorced.
   a. who's   b. whose

7. And now, I'd like to introduce the man _____ going to be our next senator . . .
   a. who's   b. whose

   . . . and his wife, _____ his greatest asset.
   c. who's   d. whose

▶ **Practice 10. Using *whose*.** (Chart 13-4)

1. Circle the possessive pronoun.
2. Draw an arrow from the possessive pronoun to the noun it refers to.
3. Replace the possessive pronoun with *whose*.
4. Combine the two sentences into one.

1. Do you know the man? His car is parked over there.

   _____

2. I know a skin doctor. His name is Dr. Skinner.

   _____

3. The people were very hospitable. We visited their home.

   _____

4. Mrs. Lake is the teacher. I enjoy her class the most.

   _____

5. The teacher asked the parents to confer with her. Their children were failing.

   _____

▶ **Practice 11. Understanding adjective clauses.** (Charts 13-1 and 13-4)
Choose the correct meanings for each sentence.

1. The secretary that trained my office assistant was arrested for ID theft.
   a. _____ My office assistant was arrested for ID theft.
   b. _____ A secretary trained my office assistant.
   c. _____ A secretary was arrested for ID theft.

2. The nurse who gave the patient her medication was unusually talkative.
   a. _____ The nurse was unusually talkative.
   b. _____ The patient was unusually talkative.
   c. _____ The patient received medication.

3. The taxi driver who turned in a lost wallet to the police received a large reward.
   a. _____ The taxi driver lost a wallet.
   b. _____ The police received a reward.
   c. _____ The taxi driver received a reward.

4. The math teacher whose methods include memorization and a focus on basic skills is very popular with parents.
   a. _____ The parents like the math teacher.
   b. _____ The parents focus on basic skills.
   c. _____ The math teacher requires memorization.

5. The computer that couldn't read your files had a virus.
   a. _____ The computer couldn't read your files.
   b. _____ The computer had a virus.
   c. _____ Your files had a virus.

6. A friend of mine whose husband is a firefighter accidentally started a fire in their kitchen.
   a. _____ My friend is a firefighter.
   b. _____ My friend started a fire.
   c. _____ The firefighter started a fire.

7. The surgeon who operated on my mother is undergoing surgery today.
   a. _____ The surgeon is having surgery today.
   b. _____ My mother is having surgery today.
   c. _____ My mother already had surgery.

▶ **Practice 12. Using *where* in adjective clauses.** (Chart 13-5)
Complete the sentences in two different ways with the given words.

1. *grew up, in, I, which, where,*
   a. The town _____ has changed.
   b. The town _____ has changed.

2. *I, where, lived, in,*
   a. The house _____ isn't there anymore.
   b. The house _____ isn't there anymore.

3. *on, lived, which, where, I*
   a. The street _____ is now a parking lot.
   b. The street _____ is now a parking lot.

4. *where, which, I, played, in*
   a. The park _____ is now a mall.
   b. The park _____ is now a mall.

▶ **Practice 13. Using *when* in adjective clauses.** (Chart 13-6)
Complete the sentences in three different ways with the given words.

1. *on, which, when, I, go, that*
   a. Saturday is the day _____ to the movies with my grandmother.
   b. Saturday is the day _____ to the movies with my grandmother.
   c. Saturday is the day _____ to the movies with my grandmother.

2. *when,   that,   which,   on,   I play tennis*

   a. Sunday is the day _____ with my friend.

   b. Sunday is the day _____ with my friend.

   c. Sunday is the day _____ with my friend.

▶ **Practice 14. Using *where* and *when* in adjective clauses.** (Charts 13-5 and 13-6)
Write the letter of the clause in the list to complete each conversation correctly.

   a. that George Washington slept in   f. which I start my new job
   b. when I spend time with my family   g. which people here celebrate their
   c. when they were really in love   independence
   d. where I was born   h. which you can do all the things you never
   e. where we can sit and talk   could before

1. A: Where do you want to go after the movie?

   B: Let's go to a place _____.

2. A: Sal and Lil broke up? That's impossible!

   B: There was a time _____, but not anymore.

3. A: See you Monday!

   B: No. Don't you remember? Monday is the day on _____.

4. A: Are you new in town?

   B: New? Are you kidding? This is the place _____.

5. A: Is there something special about that house? It looks historic.

   B: Yes. They say it's a house _____ when he was on his way to Philadelphia.

6. A: Grandma is never home. Since she's retired, she's always doing something.

   B: Right. She says that retirement is the time in _____.

7. A: What's the celebration here? Is it a holiday?

   B: Yes. It's the day on _____.

8. A: Would you like to go out this weekend?

   B: No, thanks. Saturdays and Sundays are the days _____.

▶ **Practice 15. Adjective clauses.** (Charts 13-1 → 13-6)
Circle the letter of all the words that can complete each sentence correctly.

1. Yoko told me about students _____ have taken the entrance exam 13 times.
      a. who   b. whom   c. which   d. that

2. Is this the room _____ the meeting is going to be?
      a. which   b. where   c. that   d. Ø

3. Judge Savitt is a judge _____ people respect.
      a. whose   b. which   c. whom   d. Ø

4. I'll never forget the day _____ I met Bobbi.
      a. Ø   b. that   c. when   d. which

5. We're looking for a teacher _____ specialty is teaching dyslexic children.
   a. who   b. his   c. that   d. whose

6. I'm looking for an electric can opener _____ also can sharpen knives.
   a. who   b. which   c. that   d. Ø

7. The problems _____ Tony has seem insurmountable.
   a. what   b. whom   c. that   d. Ø

8. People _____ live in glass houses shouldn't throw stones.
   a. who   b. whom   c. which   d. Ø

▶ **Practice 16. Using adjective clauses to modify pronouns.** (Chart 13-7)
Complete the sentences in Column A with a clause from Column B.

Column A	Column B
1. May I ask you a question? There is something _____.	a. who can understand Einstein's theory of relativity
2. I don't have any more money. This is all _____.	b. who doesn't mind working long hours and on weekends
3. Anyone _____ must be a genius.	c. I've been wanting to ask you
4. He's a spoiled child. His parents give him everything _____.	d. who have taken the basic course
5. I'm sorry I can't help you. There's nothing _____.	e. who had donated money to their cause
6. We need to hire someone _____.	f. that he asks for
7. The charity organization invited everyone _____.	g. that I can do about the situation
8. Students _____ can take the advanced course.	h. I have with me today

▶ **Practice 17. Punctuating adjective clauses.** (Chart 13-8)
Circle *yes* if the adjective clause requires commas and add them in the appropriate places. Circle *no* if the adjective clause does not require commas.

1. I made an appointment with a doctor who is an expert on eye disorders.   yes   (no)

2. I made an appointment with Dr. Raven, who is an expert on eye disorders.   (yes)   no

3. Bogota which is the capital of Colombia is a cosmopolitan city.   yes   no

4. The city that is the capital of Colombia is a large, cosmopolitan city.   yes   no

5. South Beach which is clean, pleasant, and fun is known as a party town.   yes   no

6. The name Bogota comes from the word *Bacata* which was the Indian name for the site.   yes   no

7. The person who writes the best essay will win a prize.   yes   no

8. The first prize was given to Belinda Jones who wrote a touching essay about being an adopted child.   yes   no

9. On our trip to Africa we visited Nairobi which is near several fascinating game reserves and then traveled to Egypt to see the pyramids.   yes   no

10. To see wild animals, you have to fly to a city that is near a game reserve and then take a small plane to the reserve itself.   yes   no

11.	Someone who understands physics better than I do is going to have to help you.	yes	no
12.	Violent tropical storms that occur in western Asia are called typhoons.	yes	no
13.	Similar storms that occur on the Atlantic side of the Americas are called hurricanes rather than typhoons.	yes	no
14.	A typhoon which is a violent tropical storm can cause great destruction.	yes	no
15.	According to the news report, the typhoon that threatened to strike the Indonesian coast has moved away from land and toward open water.	yes	no
16.	Hurricane Katrina which destroyed parts of New Orleans occurred in 2005.	yes	no

▶ **Practice 18. Punctuating adjective clauses.** (Chart 13-8)
Circle the letter of the sentence that gives the correct meaning of the given sentence.

1. The students, who attend class five hours per day, have become quite proficient in their new language.
    a. All of the students attend class five hours per day.
    b. Some of the students attend class five hours per day.

2. The students who attend class five hours per day have become quite proficient in their new language.
    a. All of the students attend class five hours per day.
    b. Some of the students attend class five hours per day.

3. The orchestra conductor signaled the violinists, who were to begin playing.
    a. All of the violinists were to begin playing.
    b. Some of the violinists were to begin playing.

4. The orchestra conductor signaled the violinists who were to begin playing.
    a. All of the violinists were to begin playing.
    b. Some of the violinists were to begin playing.

5. I put the vase on top of the TV set, which is in the living room.
    a. I have more than one TV set.
    b. I have only one TV set.

6. I put the vase on top of the TV set that is in the living room.
    a. I have more than one TV set.
    b. I have only one TV set.

7. Trees which lose their leaves in winter are called deciduous trees.
    a. All trees lose their leaves in winter.
    b. Some trees lose their leaves in winter.

8. Pine trees, which are evergreen, grow well in a cold climate.
    a. All pine trees are evergreen.
    b. Some pine trees are evergreen.

▶ **Practice 19. Using expressions of quantity in adjective clauses.** (Chart 13-9)
Combine the sentences. Use the second sentence as an adjective clause. Add commas where necessary.

1. I received two job offers. I accepted neither of them.

   _____*I received two job offers, neither of which I accepted.*_____

2. I have three brothers. Two of them are professional athletes.

   _____

3. Jerry is engaged in several business ventures. Only one of them is profitable.

   _____

4. The two women have almost completed law school. Both of them began their studies at age 40.

   _____

5. Eric is proud of his success. Much of it has been due to hard work, but some of it has been due to good luck.

   _____

6. We ordered an extra-large pizza. Half of it contained meat and half of it didn't.

   _____

7. The scientist won the Nobel Prize for his groundbreaking work. Most of his work was on genomes.

   _____

8. The audience gave a tremendous ovation to the Nobel Prize winners. Most of them were scientists.

   _____

▶ **Practice 20. Using *which* to modify a whole sentence.** (Chart 13-10)
Combine the sentences. Include an adjective clause that begins with ***which*** in the new sentence.

1. Mike was accepted at the state university. This is surprising.

   _____

2. Mike did not do well in high school. This is unfortunate.

   _____

3. The university accepts a few students each year with a low grade-point average. This is lucky for Mike.

   _____

4. The university hopes to motivate these low-performing students. This is a fine idea.

   _____

5. Mike might actually be a college graduate one day. This would be a miracle!

   _____

▶ **Practice 21. Reducing adjective clauses to adjective phrases.** (Chart 13-11)
Change the adjective clauses to adjective phrases. Cross out the adjective clause and write the adjective phrase above it.

                        wearing a green hat
1. Do you see that man ~~who is wearing a green hat~~?

2. The person who is in charge of this department is out to lunch.

3. The picture which was painted by Picasso is extremely valuable.

4. The professors who are doing research will not teach classes next year.

5. The students' research projects which are in progress must be finished by the end of the year.

6. The students' research projects which are scheduled to begin in September will have to be completed by the middle of next year.

7. Toronto, which is the largest city in Canada, is not the capital.

8. In our solar system, there are eight planets that orbit the sun.

9. Pluto, which was formerly known as a planet, was reclassified as a dwarf planet in 2006.

10. Now there is a slang verb, *to pluto,* which means "to devalue someone or something."

▶ **Practice 22. Reducing adjective clauses to adjective phrases.** (Chart 13-11)
Combine the sentences. Cross out the second sentence. Use it instead as an adjective phrase. Place the phrase in the sentence with a caret (∧). Add commas as necessary.

            ,officially inaugurated in 1960,
1. Brasilia ∧ is the capital of Brazil. ~~It was officially inaugurated in 1960.~~

2. Rio de Janeiro used to be its capital. It is the second largest city in Brazil.

3. Two languages, Finnish and Swedish, are spoken in Helsinki. It is the capital of Finland.

4. In Canada, you see signs. They are written in both English and French.

5. Libya is a leading producer of oil. It is a country in North Africa.

6. Simon Bolivar led the fight for independence early in the nineteenth century. He was a great South American general.

7. Five South American countries are Venezuela, Colombia, Ecuador, Panama, and Peru. They were liberated by Bolivar.

8. We need someone to design this project. He or she holds a degree in electrical engineering.

9. The project will be finished next year. It is being built in Beijing.

10. A lot of new buildings were constructed in Beijing in 2008. Beijing was the site of the summer Olympics that year.

▶ **Practice 23. Chapter review.**

All of the following sentences contain one or two errors in adjective clauses, adjective phrases, or punctuation. Find the errors and correct them, using a correct adjective clause or adjective phrase, and the correct punctuation.

1. When we walked past the theater, we saw a lot of people waited in a long line outside the box office.

2. Students who living on campus are close to their classrooms and the library.

3. If you need any information, see the librarian sits at the central desk on the main floor.

4. My best friend is Anna who her birthday is the same day as mine.

5. Hiroko was born in Sapporo that is a city in Japan.

6. Patrick who is my oldest brother. He is married and has one child.

7. The person sits next to me is someone I've never met him.

8. My favorite place in the world is a small city is located on the southern coast of Thailand.

9. Dr. Darnell was the only person to that I wanted to speak.

10. There are eighty students, are from all over the world, study English at this school.

11. The people who we met them on our trip last May are going to visit us in October.

12. Dianne Baxter that used to teach Spanish has organized a tour of Central America for senior citizens.

13. I've met many people since I came here who some of them are from my country.

14. People can speak English can be understood in many countries.

15. Grandpa is getting married again. This is a big surprise.

Chapter 14
Gerunds and Infinitives, Part 1

▶ **Practice 1. Gerunds: introduction.** (Chart 14-1)
Circle the gerunds. Some sentences have no gerund.

1. Driving a car is not difficult.

2. We were tired of driving, so we stopped for a rest.

3. When I saw Bob, he was driving around and looking for a parking space.

4. I enjoy singing.

5. Singing songs is a good way to learn a language.

6. Who's singing? It sounds wonderful.

▶ **Practice 2. Using gerunds as the objects of prepositions.** (Chart 14-2)
Complete the sentences with a verb from the list. Write the verb in its gerund form.

buy	fly	hear	lower
drink	go	improve	take

1. Thank you for _____ care of my plants while I was in the hospital.

2. The children are excited about _____ to the circus tomorrow.

3. Students who are interested in _____ their English conversation skills can sign up for special private classes.

4. Psychiatrists say that dreaming about _____ in the sky is quite common.

5. The candidate says he is committed to _____ taxes.

6. We are thinking about not _____ tickets for the opera this year. They have become so expensive.

7. I'm used to _____ tea with my meals. I never drink coffee.

8. We look forward to _____ from you soon.

▶ **Practice 3. Using gerunds as the objects of prepositions.** (Chart 14-2)
Complete the sentences with the correct preposition.

Part I. **Honest Henry . . .**

1. believes _____ telling the truth.

2. is not capable _____ lying.

3. never thinks _____ cheating.

4. would never forgive himself _____ cheating.

5. prohibits his children _____ lying.

Part II. **Devious Dan . . .**

6. is often guilty _____ cheating his friends.

7. never apologizes _____ cheating.

8. is accustomed _____ cheating.

9. is used _____ stealing.

10. has been accused _____ stealing.

▶ **Practice 4. Using gerunds as the objects of prepositions.** (Chart 14-2)
Write the letter of the correct preposition.

1. We are talking _____ opening a vegetarian restaurant in our neighborhood.
   a. to   b. about   c. with

2. Don't worry _____ being on time today. Everybody's going to be late because of the weather.
   a. to   b. about   c. with

3. Aren't you tired _____ studying? Let's take a break.
   a. with   b. about   c. of

4. Beth is a chocoholic. Nothing can stop her _____ eating chocolate whenever she feels like it.
   a. of   b. for   c. from

5. We are looking forward _____ seeing you again.
   a. to   b. of   c. from

6. Let's go dancing instead _____ going to the movies.
   a. with   b. about   c. of

7. Andy is still angry at me. He accused me _____ misplacing his iPod.
   a. of   b. for   c. in

8. He blames me _____ being too careless.
   a. of   b. about   c. for

9. I apologized _____ losing it, and I offered to replace it.
   a. of   b. in   c. for

10. Believe it or not, Andy is not interested _____ being my friend anymore.
    a. about   b. in   c. of

► **Practice 5. Using gerunds as the objects of prepositions.** (Chart 14-2)
Write the correct preposition and the correct form of the verb in parentheses.

1. Henry is excited _____ (*leave*) _____ for India.

2. I have no excuse _____ (*be*) _____ late.

3. The rain prevented us _____ (*complete*) _____ the work.

4. Fred is always complaining _____ (*have*) _____ a headache.

5. Instead _____ (*study*) _____, Margaret went to a ballgame with some
   of her friends.

6. The weather is terrible tonight. I don't blame you _____ (*want, not*) _____
   _____ to go to the meeting.

7. Who is responsible _____ (*wash*) _____ and
   (*dry*) _____ the dishes after dinner?

8. The thief was accused _____ (*steal*) _____ a woman's purse.

9. I'm going to visit my family during the school vacation. I'm looking forward _____
   (*eat*) _____ my mother's cooking and (*sleep*) _____ in
   my own bed.

10. I thanked my friend _____ (*lend*) _____ me lunch money.

► **Practice 6. Using gerunds as the objects of prepositions.** (Chart 14-2)
Complete the sentences with a preposition and a verb from the list. Write the verb in its gerund
form.

answer	change	live	waste
arrive	clean	save	write
buy	fail	✓ take	

1. I'm thinking _____*about taking*_____ a class in digital photography.

2. Are you interested _____ a new computer?

3. Brrr! I don't like this cold weather. I'm used _____ in warmer
   climates.

4. Please forgive me (*not*) _____ your email until now. I've been very
   busy.

5. If you are worried _____ this class, why don't you get a tutor?

6. Everybody talks _____ the situation, but nobody does anything
   about it.

7. This room is a mess! Isn't anyone responsible _____ it up?

8. Bad weather prevented the plane _____ on time.

9. Thank you _____ a letter of recommendation for me.

10. The environmental group believes _____ energy. They want to stop
    people _____ electricity.

► **Practice 7. Verbs followed by gerunds.** (Chart 14-3)
Complete the sentences with a verb from the list. Write the verb in its gerund form.

argue	have	play	sell
drive	pay	read	smoke

1. Boris' hobby is chess. He enjoys _____ chess.

2. Leon's asthma is better now. He is breathing easier since he quit _____ a year ago.

3. I don't mind _____ an hour to work every day. I always listen to a good audio book in my car.

4. I put off _____ my taxes for too long; I missed the deadline and had to pay a penalty.

5. You should avoid _____ with your boss.

6. Would you consider _____ your house at a lower price than you are asking?

7. Our teacher is so great! We really appreciate _____ a teacher like her.

8. When you finish _____ that book, may I borrow it?

► **Practice 8. *Go* + gerund.** (Chart 14-4)
Look at the pictures of the activities that the Green family and the Evans family enjoy. Use expressions in Chart 14-4 to describe the activities. Write the correct tense of *go* + a gerund.

Part I. The Green family enjoys the outdoors.

    1.   2.   3.   4.

1. Every weekend they _____ on the trails near their home.

2. In the summers they _____ on the lake. They like to go out in boats that have no motors.

3. In the winters they _____ in the mountains.

4. Last year they took a trip to Costa Rica, where they saw many colorful birds. They

   _____.

5. On that trip, they also _____ on a river.

5.

Part II. The Evans family enjoys different kinds of activities.

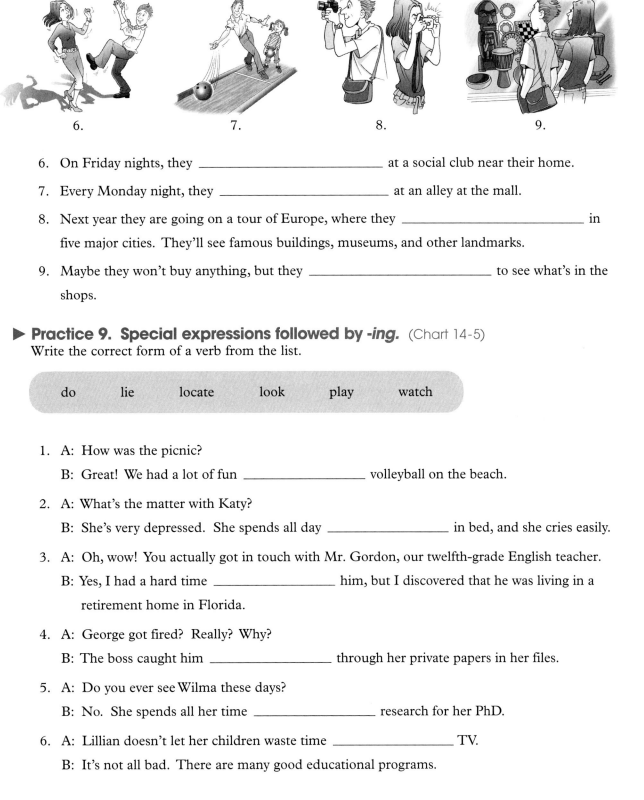

6.   7.   8.   9.

6. On Friday nights, they _____ at a social club near their home.

7. Every Monday night, they _____ at an alley at the mall.

8. Next year they are going on a tour of Europe, where they _____ in five major cities. They'll see famous buildings, museums, and other landmarks.

9. Maybe they won't buy anything, but they _____ to see what's in the shops.

▶ **Practice 9. Special expressions followed by -*ing*.** (Chart 14-5)
Write the correct form of a verb from the list.

do	lie	locate	look	play	watch

1. A: How was the picnic?
    B: Great! We had a lot of fun _____ volleyball on the beach.

2. A: What's the matter with Katy?
    B: She's very depressed. She spends all day _____ in bed, and she cries easily.

3. A: Oh, wow! You actually got in touch with Mr. Gordon, our twelfth-grade English teacher.
    B: Yes, I had a hard time _____ him, but I discovered that he was living in a retirement home in Florida.

4. A: George got fired? Really? Why?
    B: The boss caught him _____ through her private papers in her files.

5. A: Do you ever see Wilma these days?
    B: No. She spends all her time _____ research for her PhD.

6. A: Lillian doesn't let her children waste time _____ TV.
    B: It's not all bad. There are many good educational programs.

▶ **Practice 10. Verbs followed by infinitives.** (Chart 14-6)
Circle the letter of all the possible completions.

1. I want _____ that movie.
   a. to see   b. seeing   c. him to see

2. They told _____ them as soon as I got home.
   a. to call   b. calling   c. me to call

3. I expect _____ there early.
   a. to be   b. being   c. you to be

4. The police ordered _____ the building.
   a. not to enter   b. not entering   c. the people not to enter

5. We were asked _____ food and clothing for the hurricane victims.
   a. to contribute   b. contributing   c. them to contribute

6. Lisa expected _____ the lecture.
   a. to attend   b. attending   c. us to attend

▶ **Practice 11. Verbs followed by infinitives.** (Chart 14-6)
Complete the sentences with *to work* or *me to work*. Write the correct completion(s). In some cases, both are possible.

1. She hoped ____to work_____.   8. They didn't allow _____.

2. He ordered _____me to work_____.   9. You told _____.

3. We agreed _____.   10. They would like _____.

4. They wanted _____.   11. They expected _____.

5. She promised _____.   12. She decided _____.

6. They refused _____.   13. They needed _____.

7. He pretended _____.   14. They required _____.

▶ **Practice 12. Verbs followed by infinitives.** (Chart 14-6)
Rewrite each sentence. Use an infinitive phrase to make active sentences. Use the given ideas and the verbs in parentheses.

1. The teacher said to me, "You may leave early." (*permit*)

   The teacher _____.

2. The secretary said to me, "Please give this note to Sue." (*ask*)

   The secretary _____.

3. My advisor said to me, "You should take Biology 109." (*advise*)

   My advisor _____.

4. When I went to traffic court, the judge said to me, "You must pay a fine." (*order*)

   The judge _____.

5. During the test, the teacher said to Greg, "Keep your eyes on your own paper." (*warn*)

   The teacher _____.

6. During the test, the teacher said to Greg, "Don't look at your neighbor's paper." (*warn*)

   The teacher _____.

7. Mr. Lee said to the children, "Be quiet." (*tell*)

   Mr. Lee _____ .

8. When I was growing up, my parents said to me, "You may stay up late on Saturday night."

   (*allow*)

   My parents _____ .

9. The teacher said to the students, "Speak slowly and clearly." (*encourage*)

   The teacher _____ .

10. The teacher always says to the students, "You are supposed to come to class on time." (*expect*)

    The teacher _____ .

▶ **Practice 13. Verbs followed by infinitives.** (Chart 14-6)
On a separate piece of paper, rewrite each sentence in two ways. Use an infinitive phrase to make active and passive sentences with the given ideas and the verbs in parentheses. (Omit the *by*-phrase in passive sentences.)

1. The teacher said to the children, "You may go outside and play." (*allow*)
   The teacher allowed the children to go outside and play.
   The children were allowed to go outside and play.

2. The doctor said to my father, "Don't eat high-cholesterol foods." (*warn*)

3. The sergeant said to the soldiers, "March in formation." (*order*)

4. The soccer coach told the girls, "Play hard and win." (*encourage*)

5. Mary said to her roommate, "Don't forget to wake me up at 7:00." (*remind*)

6. The police officer told the drivers in our lane of traffic, "You may go ahead." (*permit*)

7. The letter said, "You must complete this form by November 15th." (*tell*)

▶ **Practice 14. Gerund or infinitive.** (Charts 14-3 and 14-6)
Write the letter of the correct completion.

1. William wants _____ us for dinner tonight.
   a. to join   b. joining

2. We offered _____ ice cream for all the children.
   a. to buy   b. buying

3. I enjoy _____ large dishes of Indian food for my friends.
   a. to cook   b. cooking

4. Avoid _____ Highway 98. There's a lot of construction going on.
   a. to take   b. taking

5. Keep on _____! Sooner or later, you'll be able to finish the puzzle.
   a. to try   b. trying

6. Would you mind _____ up the heat? It's freezing in here.
    a. to turn   b. turning

7. I pretended _____ what Irv was saying, but in reality, I didn't understand a thing.
    a. to understand   b. understand

8. Phil seems _____ in a bad mood. Do you know why?
    a. to be   b. being

9. You should consider _____ this course. It's too hard for you.
    a. to drop   b. dropping

10. Because of the stormy weather, everyone was allowed _____ work early.
    a. to leave   b. leaving

11. Students are not permitted _____ their cell phones in class.
    a. to use   b. using

12. If you quit _____ coffee, you might sleep better.
    a. to drink   b. drinking

▶ **Practice 15. Gerund or infinitive.** (Charts 14-3 and 14-6)
Circle the verb to complete the sentence correctly.

1. John doesn't mind (*to live* / *living*) alone.

2. The traffic sign warns drivers (*to be* / *being*) careful of the slippery road.

3. Travelers are required (*to show* / *showing*) their IDs at the gate.

4. Don't delay (*to make* / *making*) your reservations! Book your travel now!

5. We expect the plane (*to be* / *being*) on time.

6. I certainly appreciate (*to be* / *being*) here! Thank you for inviting me.

7. Please stop (*to hum* / *humming*) that song over and over. It bothers me.

8. My doctor suggests (*to exercise* / *exercising*) for thirty minutes every day.

9. My doctor advises (*to exercise* / *me to exercise*) for thirty minutes every day.

10. My doctor advised me (*to exercise* / *exercising*) for thirty minutes every day.

11. I was advised (*to exercise* / *exercising*) for thirty minutes every day by my doctor.

12. I advised (*to consult* / *my friend to consult*) a lawyer.

13. My friend was advised (*to consult* / *consulting*) a lawyer.

14. She asked me (*to recommend* / *recommending*) a good lawyer.

▶ **Practice 16. Gerund or infinitive.** (Charts 14-3 and 14-6)

Complete the sentences with the gerund or infinitive form of the verb in **bold**. Use *him* if a pronoun is required.

Part I. Complete the sentences with *stay*.

1. I expect _____.
2. I want _____.
3. I forced _____.
4. I invited _____.
5. I considered _____.
6. I told _____.
7. I was told _____.
8. I refused _____.
9. I encouraged _____.
10. I would like _____.

Part II. Complete the sentences with *travel*.

1. He doesn't mind _____.
2. He enjoys _____.
3. He needed _____.
4. He quit _____.
5. He is allowed _____.
6. He put off _____.
7. He recommends _____.
8. He can't stand _____.
9. He finished _____.
10. He mentioned _____.

Part III. Complete the sentences with *work*.

1. They discussed _____.
2. They intend _____.
3. They were ordered _____.
4. They decided _____.
5. They offered _____.
6. They delayed _____.
7. They required _____.
8. They hope _____.
9. They plan _____.
10. They avoided _____.

▶ **Practice 17. Gerund or infinitive.** (Chart 14-7)

Complete the sentences with the gerund or infinitive form of the verb.

1. Don't forget (*turn*) _____ off your computers before you leave the office.

2. I'll never forget (*meet*) _____ the president when I was a child.

3. I'll remember (*stop*) _____ at the grocery store if I write myself a note and stick it in the window of my car.

4. Do you remember (*see*) _____ a man running out of the bank with a large bag in his hand?

5. Don't give me any more advice. Please stop (*tell*) _____ me what to do.

6. At the mall, I met my old English teacher. We stopped (*talk*) _____ for a while. That was very pleasant.

7. I had a bad argument with my friend Jerry two years ago. We stopped (*speak*) _____ then and haven't spoken since.

8. We regret (*buy*) _____ this house. It needs too many repairs.

9. The letter said, "I regret (*tell*) _____ you that your application has been denied."

10. I tried very hard (*learn*) _____ Chinese, but I couldn't do it. I am just not good at languages.

11. We don't know how to communicate with that man. We've tried (*talk*) _____ to him in Spanish, we've tried in Greek, we've tried in German, and we've tried in French. So far nothing's worked.

▶ **Practice 18. Gerund or infinitive.** (Chart 14-7)

Circle the letter of the sentence that has the same meaning as the given sentence.

1. Jean and her husband stopped drinking coffee.
   a. They had a cup of coffee together.
   b. They don't drink coffee anymore.

2. I regret to tell you that your aunt is very ill.
   a. I am sorry to inform you that your aunt is very ill.
   b. I am sorry that I informed you that your aunt was very ill.

3. Rita remembers locking the door this morning.
   a. Rita never forgets to lock the door in the morning.
   b. Rita remembers that she locked the door this morning.

4. I forgot to call my grandmother.
   a. I didn't call my grandmother.
   b. I don't remember whether I called my grandmother or not.

5. My back was sore from being at the computer all morning. I stopped to rest.
   a. I kept working.
   b. I took a break.

▶ **Practice 19. Gerund or infinitive.** (Chart 14-7)

Circle the letter of the correct completions. In some sentences, both are correct.

1. It was raining hard, but we continued _____.
   a. to drive   b. driving

2. The veterinarian tried _____ the horse's life, but he failed.
   a. to save   b. saving

3. As soon as the play ended, the audience began _____ wildly.
   a. to applaud   b. applauding

4. I prefer _____ a movie rather than see one in a theater.
   a. to rent   b. renting

5. I prefer _____ movies at home.
   a. to see   b. seeing

6. I hate _____ in the house when the weather is beautiful.
   a. to stay   b. staying

7. I love ____ on the beach.
    a. to walk   b. walking

8. Most people enjoy ____ to music.
    a. to listen   b. listening

9. When you finish ____, call me and I'll come to pick you up.
    a. to shop   b. shopping

10. Please don't cry. I can't stand ____ you cry.
    a. to see   b. seeing

▶ **Practice 20. It + infinitive; gerunds and infinitives as subjects.** (Charts 14-8)
Circle the correct word or phrase in parentheses.

1. (*Is / It's*) easy to use a computer.

2. Using a computer (*is / it's*) easy.

3. To speak another language (*is not / it's not*) easy.

4. (*Is it / Is*) difficult to speak another language?

5. (*Go / Going*) dancing is fun.

6. (*It's / Is*) fun to go dancing.

7. Traveling (*is / it's*) sometimes tiring.

8. It's dangerous (*jump / to jump*) out of airplanes in a parachute.

9. (*See / To see*) the Grand Canyon is a thrilling experience.

10. (*Is / Is it*) collecting coins an interesting hobby?

▶ **Practice 21. Review.** (Charts 14-2 → 14-8)
Circle the letter of all the possible completions.

1. ____ to play tennis.

    a. I would like   g. I told Ted

    b. I asked Jack   h. We discussed

    c. I'm thinking about   i. It's a good day

    d. I invited Ann   j. I enjoyed

    e. We had fun   k. We began

    f. I suggested   l. I hope

2. ____ playing tennis early.

    a. We finished   g. I promised Fred

    b. We want   h. We stopped

    c. I want them   i. I was invited

    d. We quit   j. We tried

    e. It's a lovely day   k. We recommended

    f. I'm interested in   l. We considered

▶ **Practice 22. Gerund or infinitive.** (Charts 14-9 and 14-10)
Write the letter of the correct completion.

1. Air travelers have to anticipate _____ in long lines.
    a. to wait   b. waiting

2. The electronics store agreed _____ back the damaged radio.
    a. to take   b. taking

3. Doctor, would you mind _____ me the information in language I can understand?
    a. to give   b. giving

4. I miss _____ you in class every day.
    a. to see   b. seeing

5. Dan failed _____ the firefighter's examination and was quite upset.
    a. to pass   b. passing

6. The bad weather caused us _____ our connecting flight to Rome.
    a. to miss   b. missing

7. We dislike _____ dinner at 9:00 P.M.
    a. to eat   b. eating

8. Most of the students finished _____ their research papers on time.
    a. to write   b. writing

9. My niece hopes _____ with me to Disneyland next April.
    a. to go   b. going

10. This note will remind me _____ the chicken for dinner tomorrow night.
    a. to defrost   b. defrosting

11. Billy denied _____ the whole bag of potato chips that was on the table.
    a. to eat   b. eating

12. In a court of law, you must swear _____ the truth, the whole truth, and nothing but the truth.
    a. to tell   b. telling

13. I'm sorry. I didn't mean _____ you.
    a. to frighten   b. frightening

14. I regret not _____ harder when I was in high school.
    a. to study   b. studying

► **Practice 23. Review.** (Chapter 14)

Write the correct form of a verb from the list.

apply	end	operate	run	speak	use
camp	get	read	sleep	turn	watch

1. Our family goes _____ in the summer and fall. We love to cook outdoors and sleep in tents under the stars.

2. The doctor was forced _____ immediately to save the patient's life.

3. I have to drive more carefully. I can't risk _____ another speeding ticket.

4. Think about _____ for that new job. You can do it, I know.

5. The sign at the intersection warns drivers not _____ right when the light is red.

6. When Bess entered the room, she found her two cats _____ on her bed.

7. When you get through _____ the newspaper, could you please give me a little help in the kitchen?

8. I was furious at Bill's rude behavior. I threatened _____ our friendship.

9. Bill regretted _____ rude language and apologized for _____ to me in the way that he did.

10. The customers at the bank just stood _____ helplessly as a masked gunman held everyone at gunpoint.

11. But two police officers caught the gunman _____ out of the bank carrying two large bags of money.

► **Practice 24. Chapter review.**

Correct the errors. All the errors are in the use of gerunds and infinitives and the words that go with them.

1. I don't enjoy to watch TV.

2. I prefer to spend time to play board games and computer games.

3. It's important keep your mind active.

4. There is some evidence that older people can avoid to become senile by exercise their brain.

5. Playing word games it is one good way to stimulate your brain.

6. In addition, is beneficial for everyone to exercise regularly.

7. Doctors advise older people eating fish two or three times a week.

8. Everyone should try eat well and exercise every day.

9. Pedro is interested to learn about other cultures.

10. He wants live in Japan next year.

11. He's excited about attend a university there.

12. Right now he is struggling learning Japanese.

13. He has a hard time to pronounce the words.

14. He keeps on to study and to practice.

15. At night, he lies in bed to listen to Japanese language-teaching programs.

16. Then he dreams to travel to Japan.

Chapter **15**
Gerunds and Infinitives, Part 2

▶ **Practice 1. Infinitive of purpose: *in order to.*** (Chart 15-1)
Correct the errors. Not every sentence has an error.

David is in Mexico . . . .

1. for visit

2. for a convention

3. for his cousin's wedding

4. to go sightseeing

5. for learn Spanish

6. to his health

7. for see the Mayan ruins

8. for the cool mountain air

▶ **Practice 2. Infinitive of purpose: *in order to.*** (Chart 15-1)
Circle the letter of the correct completion. In some sentences, both are correct.

1. Emily likes _____ ice skating every weekend.
   a. to go   b. in order to go

2. Darcy opened the door _____ some fresh air in.
   a. to let   b. in order to let

3. Beth practices night and day _____ ready for her piano recital next month.
   a. to be   b. in order to be

4. Sue sent me an email _____ me that the meeting had been canceled.
   a. to inform   b. in order to inform

5. We've decided not _____ a vacation this year.
   a. to take   b. in order to take

6. Did you remember _____ Mr. Johnson?
   a. to call   b. in order to call

7. On nice summer nights, we often walk on the beach _____ the sunsets.
   a. to watch   b. in order to watch

8. The boys were so noisy that I had to ring a loud bell _____ their attention.
   a. to get   b. in order to get

9. Airport workers wear ear protectors _____ their ears from jet noise.
   a. to protect   b. in order to protect

► **Practice 3. Adjectives followed by infinitives.** (Chart 15-2)
Complete the conversations. Write the letter of the phrase from the list.

a. to hear that
b. to bring the paper cups and paper plates
c. to get into one

d. to be alive
e. to introduce our country's president
f. to lose the next game

1. A: Marta had a bad accident, I heard.

   B: Yes, she did. She's lucky _____.

2. A: Why does Mr. Carlin walk up twelve flights of stairs every day? Is it for the exercise?

   B: No, not at all. He has a phobia about elevators. He's afraid _____.

3. A: Who is going to cook dinner for our next meeting?

   B: I can't cook, but I'm willing _____.

4. A: Our dog died.

   B: Oh, that's a shame. I'm very sorry _____.

5. A: Our three best soccer players are out with injuries.

   B: I know. Without them, you're likely _____.

6. A: Turn the volume up. I want to hear what the senator is saying.

   B: "Ladies and gentlemen, I am proud _____."

► **Practice 4. Using infinitives with *too* and *very*.** (Chart 15-3)
Write ***very*** or ***too*** to complete each sentence correctly.

1. The box is _____very_____ heavy, but I can lift it.

2. John dropped his physics course because it was _____ difficult for him.

3. I think it's _____ late to get tickets to the concert. I heard they were all sold
   out.

4. Peter has turned 20. Now he's _____ old to take part in the ski races for
   teenagers.

5. Nancy was _____ ill. Nevertheless, she came to the family reunion.

6. Learning a second language can be _____ difficult, but most students in the
   class are doing well.

7. Professor Andrews is always _____ interesting, but I'm _____
   tired to go to the lecture tonight.

8. Phil is _____ young to understand. He'll understand when he's older.

9. I'm _____ sleepy to watch the rest of the TV movie. Let me know how it turns
   out in the end.

10. A: I like your pin. It looks antique.

    B: It is. It's _____ old. It belonged to my great-grandmother.

► **Practice 5. Using infinitives with *too* and *enough*.** (Chart 15-3)
Write *very*, *too*, or *enough* to complete each sentence correctly.

1. The classroom is _____*very*_____ small, but it's big _____*enough*_____ to hold fifteen students.

2. It's _____ dark to see in here. Please turn on the lights.

3. There's not _____ light in here. Can you turn on another light?

4. These new windows are made of specially treated glass. The glass is _____ strong. It's strong _____ to resist the strong winds of hurricanes.

5. We'd like to go out in our sailboat today because the weather is _____ nice. However, there isn't _____ wind to sail.

6. A trip to Europe is _____ expensive for our family this year. We don't have _____ money to travel this year.

7. You're _____ young to drive a car, Emily. You're only twelve years old! There will be time _____ to drive when you're older.

8. Dinner was _____ good. This restaurant is good _____ to come back to.

9. It's _____ hot today, but I'm going to take my daily walk anyway.

10. It's hot _____ to fry an egg on the sidewalk!

► **Practice 6. Passive infinitives and gerunds.** (Chart 15-4)
Complete the sentences with the passive form of the verbs in parentheses.

1. I hope (*accepted*) _____ at State College.

2. I would like (*given*) _____ a scholarship.

3. Leo wants (*picked*) _____ for the soccer team.

4. Cats enjoy (*petted*) _____.

5. Babies need (*held*) _____.

6. I really appreciate (*invited*) _____ to join this group.

7. Al is shy. He avoids (*noticed*) _____.

8. Harold mentioned (*invited*) _____ to a dinner at his boss's house.

► **Practice 7. Passive infinitives and gerunds.** (Chart 15-4)
Choose the infinitive or the passive infinitive. Write the letter of the correct completion.

1. The mail is supposed _____ before noon.
   a. to deliver   b. to be delivered

2. The mail carrier is supposed _____ the mail before noon.
   a. to deliver   b. to be delivered

3. Janice is going to fill out an application. She wants _____ for the job.
   a. to consider   b. to be considered

4. I expect _____ at the airport by my uncle.
   a. to meet   b. to be met

5. Mr. Steinberg offered _____ us to the train station.
   a. to drive   b. to be driven

6. The children appear _____ about the trip.
   a. to excite   b. to be excited

7. My co-worker and I agreed _____ the work equally.
   a. to divide   b. to be divided

8. Our boss appears _____ with this arrangement.
   a. to please   b. to be pleased

▶ **Practice 8. Passive infinitives and gerunds.** (Chart 15-4)
Choose the gerund or the passive gerund. Write the letter of the correct completion.

1. Shhh! Don't ask questions! The professor doesn't appreciate _____ when he's speaking.
   a. interrupting   b. being interrupted

2. Avoid _____ Highway 77. There are a lot of delays because of construction.
   a. taking   b. being taken

3. The mountain climbers are in danger of _____ by an avalanche.
   a. killing   b. being killed

4. Does Dr. Johnson mind _____ at home if his patients need his help?
   a. calling   b. being called

5. I'm interested in _____ my conversational skills.
   a. improving   b. being improved

6. When Alex got home from school, he didn't mention _____ by his teacher.
   a. scolding   b. being scolded

7. Sally's low test scores kept her from _____ to the university.
   a. admitting   b. being admitted

8. Mr. Miller gave no indication of _____ his mind.
   a. changing   b. being changed

▶ **Practice 9. Passive infinitives and gerunds.** (Chart 15-4)
Complete the sentences with the correct form of the verbs in parentheses.

1. We turn off the phone during dinner. We don't want (*call*) _____

   at that time.

2. Not many people enjoy (*call*) _____ by salespeople.

3. Each candidate hopes (*elect*) _____ by a large majority of the people.

4. It's not easy (*elect*) _____.

5. Our mayor has an excellent chance (*re-elect*) _____.

6. Sometimes teenagers complain about not (*understand*) _____ by

   their parents.

7. Sometimes teenagers would like just (*leave*) _____ alone.

8. Don't all of us want (*love*) _____ and (*need*) _____ by other people?

▶ **Practice 10. Using gerunds or passive infinitives following *need*.** (Chart 15-5)
Circle the letters of all the sentences that can follow the given sentence.

1. A lot of things in our house don't work.
   a. We need to repair them.
   b. They need to repair.
   c. They need to be repaired.
   d. They need repairing.

2. The refrigerator is so old that it hardly works anymore.
   a. We need to replace the refrigerator.
   b. It needs to replace.
   c. It needs to be replaced.
   d. It needs replacing.

3. The sink has been leaking for a month.
   a. A plumber needs to fix the sink.
   b. The sink needs to fix.
   c. The sink needs to be fixed.
   d. The sink needs fixing.

4. The color of the walls has faded.
   a. We need to paint the walls.
   b. The walls need to paint.
   c. The walls need to be painted.
   d. The walls need painting.

5. We don't have a good repair person.
   a. We need to find a good repair person.
   b. A good repair person needs to find.
   c. A good repair person needs to be found.
   d. We need a repair person to find.

6. Please tell your repair person to call me.
   a. I need to call your repair person.
   b. I need to be called by your repair person.
   c. Your repair person needs to call me.
   d. Your repair person needs calling.

▶ **Practice 11. Using verbs of perception.** (Chart 15-6)
Complete the sentences with a verb from the list. Use each word only once. Use the simple form or the *-ing* form, whichever seems better to you. Sometimes both are OK.

arrive	do	pass	reach	talk
cry	leave	practice	rock	win

1. Whenever I can, I like to watch the basketball team _____ for the upcoming game.

2. It's interesting to sit in the airport and watch all the people _____ by.

3. I heard an upset baby _____.

4. Did you see Charles _____ the office? He ran out in a really big hurry!

5. It was a thrill to see my brother _____ the chess tournament last year.

6. I was amazed to see the firefighters _____ so soon after my call.

7. I can't stand to be on a boat. When I feel the boat _____, I get seasick.

8. When I watch my yoga instructor _____ the exercises, it seems easy, but when I try them, it is hard.

9. We listened to the newscaster _____ about the oncoming tornadoes.

10. A security guard at the bank observed a suspicious-looking man _____
into his pocket for something. The guard thought it was a gun, but it turned out to be the
man's asthma inhaler.

▶ **Practice 12. Using the simple form after *let* and *help*.** (Chart 15-7)
Write the letter of the correct completion. More than one completion may be correct. If so, write
both.

1. The school guard stopped all the traffic to let the children _____ the street.
  a. cross   b. to cross   c. crossing

2. My friend Ole is very relaxed. He never lets anything _____ him.
  a. to bother   b. bother   c. bothering

3. My daughter helped me _____ an application online.
  a. filling out   b. filled out   c. fill out

4. Will you please help me _____ the kitchen? Otherwise, I'll be here all night!
  a. clean up   b. to clean up   c. cleaning up

5. Elsa used to have very short hair, but now it is longer. She is letting it _____.
  a. growing   b. to grow   c. grow

6. We don't let our dog _____ around outside. We always take him for walks on a leash.
  a. run   b. to run   c. running

7. Is it true that if you eat fish every day, it will help you _____ smarter?
  a. to become   b. becoming   c. become

8. Did someone help you _____ this research paper?
  a. write   b. wrote   c. writing

▶ **Practice 13. Using causative verbs: *make, have, get*.** (Chart 15-8)
Complete the sentences with the correct form of the verbs in parentheses.

1. The general made the soldiers (*stand*) _____ at attention.

2. Don't get rid of those shoes just because they are old. Have them (*fix*) _____
at the shoe repair shop.

3. Exercise makes your heart (*beat*) _____ faster.

4. What can we do to get Marissa (*stop*) _____ smoking?

5. Jean finally got her son (*clean*) _____ his room.

6. Paula's new haircut makes her (*look*) _____ ten years younger.

7. I'm sorry, sir. Your prescription is not renewable. Have your physician
(*call*) _____ us here at the pharmacy, and then we can refill
it for you.

8. Please take this document to the copy store and have 15 copies
(*make*) _____. There are 150 pages, so you'd better have
spiral bindings (*put*) _____ on too.

▶ **Practice 14. Using causative verbs: *make, have, get.*** (Chart 15-8)
Circle the letter of the correct completions. More than one completion may be correct.

1. You can ____ the bookstore order some books for you.
   a. make   b. have   c. get

2. You can order your books from the online bookstore and ____ them sent to you.
   a. make   b. have   c. get

3. If you're nice to James, maybe you can ____ him to drive you to the airport.
   a. make   b. have   c. get

4. I'll ____ the taxi driver take me to the airport.
   a. make   b. have   c. get

5. The comedian is so funny. I can't help laughing even though I'm sad. That comedian can
   ____ anyone laugh.
   a. make   b. have   c. get

6. The students tried to ____ the professor to postpone the exam, but he didn't.
   a. make   b. have   c. get

7. I'm going to ____ my car washed on Saturday.
   a. make   b. have   c. get

8. Ms. Andrews isn't there? ____ her call me, please.
   a. Make   b. Have   c. Get

9. A magician can ____ a rabbit appear and disappear.
   a. make   b. have   c. get

▶ **Practice 15. Verb form review.** (Chapters 14 and 15)
Circle the letter of the correct completion.

1. I enjoy ____ to the park on summer evenings.
   a. to go   b. going   c. being gone   d. go

2. Don't forget ____ home as soon as you arrive at your destination.
   a. to call   b. calling   c. call   d. to be called

3. When we kept getting unwanted calls, I called the phone company and had my phone number
   ____ .
   a. change   b. changed   c. to change   d. changing

4. Jean should seriously consider ____ an actress. She is a very talented performer.
   a. to become   b. become   c. becoming   d. will become

5. ____ television to the exclusion of all other activities is not a healthy habit for a growing child.
   a. Watch   b. Being watched   c. Watching   d. To be watched

6. After their children had grown up, Mr. and Mrs. Sills decided ____ to a condominium in the
   city. They've never been sorry.
   a. moved   b. moving   c. move   d. to move

7. Are you interested in ____ the movie at University Theater?
   a. see   b. to see   c. being seen   d. seeing

8. The store manager caught the cashier _____ money from the cash register and promptly called the police. They discovered that it had been going on for a long time.
    a. to steal   b. stealing   c. stole   d. being stolen

9. The municipal authorities advised us _____ all drinking water during the emergency.
    a. to boil   b. to be boiled   c. boiling   d. boil

10. If we leave now for our trip, we can drive half the distance before we stop _____ lunch.
    a. having   b. to have   c. have   d. for having

11. It was difficult _____ the dialogue in the movie. The acoustics in the theater were very bad.
    a. to hear   b. hearing   c. heard   d. to heard

12. Our school basketball team won the championship game by _____ two points in the last five seconds. It was the most exciting game I have ever attended.
    a. being scored   b. to score   c. scoring   d. score

13. The flight attendants made all the passengers _____ their seat belts during the turbulence.
    a. to buckle   b. buckling   c. to buckled   d. buckle

14. At our class reunion, we had a lot of fun _____ at pictures of ourselves from twenty years ago.
    a. looking   b. look   c. looked   d. to look

15. It has become necessary _____ water in the metropolitan area because of the severe drought.
    a. rationing   b. ration   c. have rationed   d. to ration

▶ **Practice 16. Verb form review.** (Chapters 14 and 15)
Complete the sentences with the correct form of the verb in parentheses. Some sentences are passive.

1. Bill decided (*buy*) _____ a new car rather than a used one.

2. We delayed (*open*) _____ the doors of the testing center until exactly 9:00.

3. I really dislike (*ask*) _____ to answer questions in class when I haven't prepared my lesson.

4. I certainly didn't anticipate (*have*) _____ to wait in line for three hours for tickets to the baseball game!

5. When I was younger, I used (*wear*) _____ mini-skirts and bright colors. Now I am accustomed to (*dress*) _____ more conservatively.

6. Skydivers must have nerves of steel. I can't imagine (*jump*) _____ out of a plane and (*fall*) _____ to the earth. What if the parachute didn't open?

7. We are looking forward to (*take*) _____ on a tour of Athens by our Greek friends.

8. I told the mail carrier that we would be away for two weeks on vacation. I asked her (*stop*) _____ (*deliver*) _____ our mail until the 21st. She told me (*fill*) _____ out a form at the post office so that the post office would hold our mail until we returned.

9. The elderly man next door is just sitting in his rocking chair (*gaze*) _____ out the window. I wish there were something I could do (*cheer*) _____ him up.

10. I resent (*have*) _____ to work on this project with Fred. I know I'll end up with most of the work falling on my shoulders.

▶ **Practice 17. Review.** (Chapters 14 and 15)
Circle the letter of the correct form of the verb to complete each sentence.

1. Alice didn't expect ____ to Bill's party.
   a. to ask   b. to be asked   c. asking

2. Matthew left the office without ____ anyone.
   a. tell   b. telling   c. told

3. It's useless. Give up. Enough's enough. Don't keep ____ your head against a brick wall.
   a. beat   b. beating   c. to beat

4. I hope ____ a scholarship for the coming semester.
   a. to award   b. to be awarded   c. being awarded

5. We are very pleased ____ your invitation.
   a. to accept   b. to be accepted   c. accept

6. It was exciting ____ to faraway places last year.
   a. travel   b. to travel   c. to traveled

7. Conscientious parents don't let their children ____ too much television.
   a. watch   b. to watch   c. watching

8. Did you see that deer ____ across the road?
   a. run   b. ran   c. to run

9. Mr. Carson was very lucky ____ to represent the company in Paris.
   a. to be chosen   b. choosing   c. to chose

10. Last Saturday, we went ____ .
    a. to shop   b. shopping   c. to shopping

11. ____ in the mountains is Tom's favorite activity.
    a. Hike   b. Hiking   c. Go to hike

12. The physical activity makes him ____ good.
    a. feel   b. to feel   c. feeling

13. Martha opened the window ____ in some fresh air.
    a. let   b. letting   c. to let

14. Scott wastes a lot of time ____ out with his friends at the mall.
    a. hanging   b. to hang   c. hang

15. Did you remember ____ the front door?
    a. lock   b. to lock   c. locking

16. I don't remember ever ____ that story before.
    a. hearing   b. heard   c. to hear

17. You should stop ____ if you get sleepy.
    a. drive   b. driving   c. to drive

18. I have trouble _____ asleep at night.
    a. fall   b. to fall   c. falling

19. After driving for three hours, we stopped _____ something to eat.
    a. to get   b. getting   c. got

20. The refrigerator needs _____ again.
    a. fixing   b. to fix   c. fixed

21. That pan is really hot. It's too hot _____ up without an oven mitt.
    a. pick   b. picking   c. to pick

▶ **Practice 18. Verb form review.** (Chapters 14 and 15)
Correct the errors.

1. You shouldn't let children playing with matches.

2. Bobby was lying in bed to cry.

3. You can get there more quickly by take River Road instead of the interstate highway.

4. Isabel expected being admitted to the university, but she wasn't.

5. Our lawyer advised us not signing the contract until she had a chance to study it very carefully.

6. John was responsible for to notify everyone about the meeting.

7. Apparently, he failed to calling several people.

8. I couldn't understand what the passage said, so I asked my friend translated it for me.

9. You can find out the meaning of the word by look it up in a dictionary.

10. No, that's not what I meant to say. How can I make you understanding?

11. Serena wore a large hat for protect her face from the sun.

12. We like to go to fish on weekends.

13. Maybe you can get Charlie taking you to the airport.

14. My doctor advised me not eating food with a high fat content.

15. Doctors always advise eat less and exercising more.

16. Allen smelled something to burn. When he ran into the kitchen, he saw fire coming out of the oven.

Chapter 16
Coordinating Conjunctions

▶ **Practice 1. Parallel structure.** (Chart 16-1)
Write the letter of the correct completion.

1. In the winter, Iceland is cold and _____.
   a. ice   b. dark   c. a country

2. Dan opened the door and _____ the room.
   a. enter   b. entering   c. entered

3. This dish is made of meat, potatoes, and _____.
   a. spicy   b. salty   c. vegetables

4. Jerry was driving and _____ on the phone at the same time.
   a. talks   b. talking   c. talked

5. Mimi learned how to sing and _____ at the Academy of the Arts.
   a. danced   b. dancing   c. dance

6. I have written and _____ her, but I have received no response.
   a. call   b. calling   c. called

7. Somebody called and _____ up.
   a. hung   b. hang   c. hanging

8. Don't call and _____ up. Leave a short message.
   a. hung   b. hang   c. hanging

▶ **Practice 2. Parallel structure.** (Chart 16-1)
Circle the conjunction that joins the parallel words. Then <u>underline</u> the words that are parallel and circle the letter of the part of speech that describes them.

1. These apples are <u>fresh</u> (and) <u>sweet</u>.
   (a.) adjective   d. adverb
   b. noun   e. gerund
   c. verb   f. infinitive

2. These apples and pears are fresh.
   a. adjective   d. adverb
   b. noun   e. gerund
   c. verb   f. infinitive

3. I washed and dried the apples.
   a. adjective   d. adverb
   b. noun   e. gerund
   c. verb   f. infinitive

4. I am washing and drying the apples.
      a. adjective   d. adverb
      b. noun   e. gerund
      c. verb   f. infinitive

5. We ate the fruit happily and quickly.
      a. adjective   d. adverb
      b. noun   e. gerund
      c. verb   f. infinitive

6. Those imported apples are delicious but expensive.
      a. adjective   d. adverb
      b. noun   e. gerund
      c. verb   f. infinitive

7. Apples, pears, and bananas are kinds of fruit.
      a. adjective   d. adverb
      b. noun   e. gerund
      c. verb   f. infinitive

8. I like an apple or a banana with my cereal.
      a. adjective   d. adverb
      b. noun   e. gerund
      c. verb   f. infinitive

9. Those apples are red, ripe, and juicy.
      a. adjective   d. adverb
      b. noun   e. gerund
      c. verb   f. infinitive

▶ **Practice 3. Parallel structure.** (Chart 16-1)
Write the letter of the word or phrase that best completes the sentence.

   a. carefully   e. reliable health care
   b. excellence in   f. responsible
   c. in agriculture   g. seeking practical solutions
   d. provide quality education   h. finds a way to get the important jobs done

1. Mr. Li has had wide experience. He has worked in business, in the news media, and _____.

2. People want safe homes, good schools, and _____.

3. As a taxpayer, I want my money used wisely and _____.

4. Mrs. Adams is respected for researching issues and _____.

5. Ms. Hunter has established a record of effective and _____ leadership in government.

6. She has worked hard to control excess government spending, protect our environment, and

   _____.

7. Carol is a hard-working personnel manager who welcomes challenges and _____.

8. I will continue to fight for adequate funding of and _____ education.

▶ **Practice 4. Parallel structure: using commas.** (Chart 16-2)
Add commas as necessary.

1. Jack was calm and quiet.

2. Jack was calm quiet and serene.

3. The football players practiced kicking and throwing the ball and they ran laps.

4. The football players practiced kicking throwing and running.

5. The children collected rocks and insects, and flew kites.

6. The teacher told the children to sit down be quiet and open their reading books.

7. The teacher told the children to sit down and be quiet.

8. Did you know that the pupil of your eye expands and — pupil
contracts slightly with each heartbeat?

9. Our server carried two cups of coffee three glasses of water one glass of orange juice and three orders of eggs on her tray.

10. My parents were strict but fair with their children.

▶ **Practice 5. Parallel structure.** (Charts 16-1 and 16-2)
<u>Underline</u> the words that are supposed to be parallel. Write "C" if the parallel structure is correct. Write "I" if the parallel structure is incorrect, and make any necessary corrections.

1. __I__ I admire him for his <u>intelligence</u>, cheerful <u>disposition</u>, and ~~he is honest~~. *honesty*

2. __C__ Abraham Lincoln was a <u>lawyer</u> and a <u>politician</u>.

3. _____ The boat sailed across the lake smoothly and quiet.

4. _____ Barb studies each problem carefully and works out a solution.

5. _____ Aluminum is plentiful and relatively inexpensive.

6. _____ Many visitors to Los Angeles enjoy visiting Disneyland and to tour movie studios.

7. _____ Children are usually interested in but a little frightened by snakes.

8. _____ So far this term, the students in the writing class have learned how to write thesis statements, organize their material, and summarizing their conclusions.

9. _____ When I looked more closely, I saw that it was not coffee but chocolate on my necktie.

10. _____ Physics explains why water freezes and how the sun produces heat.

11. _____ All plants need light, a suitable climate, and they require an ample supply of water and minerals from the soil.

12. _____ With their keen sight, fine hearing, and refined sense of smell, wolves hunt day or night in quest of elk, deer, moose, or caribou.

▶ **Practice 6. Paired conjunctions:** *both . . . and; not only . . . but also; either . . . or; neither . . . nor.* (Chart 16-3)

Complete the sentences with the correct present tense form of the verb in parentheses.

1. Neither the students nor the teacher (*know*) _____knows_____ the answer.

2. Neither the teacher nor the students (*know*) _____know_____ the answer.

3. Not only the students but also the teacher (*know*) _____ the answer.

4. Not only the teacher but also the students (*know*) _____ the answer.

5. Both the teacher and the students (*know*) _____ the answer.

6. Neither Alan nor Carol (*want*) _____ to go skiing this weekend.

7. Both John and Ted (*like*) _____ to go cross-country skiing.

8. Either Jack or Alice (*have*) _____ the information you need.

9. Neither my parents nor my brother (*agree*) _____ with my decision.

10. Both intelligence and skill (*be*) _____ essential to good teaching.

11. Neither my classmates nor my teacher (*realize*) _____ that I have no idea what's going on in class.

12. Not only my husband but also my children (*be*) _____ in favor of my decision to return to school and finish my graduate degree.

▶ **Practice 7. Paired conjunctions:** *both . . . and; not only . . . but also; either . . . or; neither . . . nor.* (Chart 16-3)

Write sentences with the given words and the paired conjunctions. Use capital letters and punctuation where necessary.

1. Mary drinks coffee. Her parents drink coffee.

   a. both . . . and _____.

   b. neither . . . nor _____.

2. John will do the work. Henry will do the work.

   a. either . . . or _____.

   b. neither . . . nor _____.

3. Our school recycles trash. The restaurants in town recycle trash.

   a. not only . . . but also _____.

   b. both . . . and _____.

▶ **Practice 8. Paired conjunctions:** *both . . . and; not only . . . but also; either . . . or; neither . . . nor.* (Chart 16-3)

Part I. Use *both . . . and*.

1. You know her mother. Do you know her father too?

   Yes, I know _____both her mother and her father_____.

2. The nurses usually arrive early. Does the doctor arrive early too?

   Yes, _____ early.

3. Bananas originated in Asia. Did mangos originate in Asia too?

Yes, _____ in Asia.

4. Whales are mammals. Are dolphins mammals too?

Yes, _____ mammals.

Part II. Use *not only . . . but also*.

5. Ethiopia exports coffee. Does it export oil too?

Ethiopia _____.

6. Air Greenland flies to Greenland. What about Icelandair?

_____ to Greenland.

7. You bought a lime-green jacket. What about pants? Did you buy lime-green pants too?

Yes, I bought _____ to go with it.

8. Al attended Harvard University. Did he attend Harvard Law School too?

Yes, Al _____.

Part III. Use *either . . . or*.

9. Someone knows the answer. Is it Ricky? Paula? One of them knows.

_____ the answer.

10. You're going to Mexico on your vacation. Are you going to Costa Rica too?

We're going _____, not to both.

11. Who will take Taka to the airport: Jim or Taka's parents?

_____ to the airport.

12. Helen's buying salmon. Is she buying tuna too?

No. She's buying _____, whichever looks fresher.

Part IV. Use *neither . . . nor*.

13. Fred doesn't eat red meat. Do his children eat red meat?

No, _____ eat red meat.

14. She doesn't have health insurance. Do her children have health insurance?

No, _____ health insurance.

15. Luis doesn't have a family. Does he have friends?

No, _____.

16. How's the weather there? Is it hot? Is it cold?

It's perfect! It's _____.

▶ **Practice 9. Separating independent clauses with periods; connecting them with *and* and *but*.** (Chart 16-4)

Punctuate the sentences by adding commas or periods. Do not add any words. Add capitalization as necessary.

1. The rain stopped the birds sang.

2. The rain stopped and the birds sang.

3. The rain stopped the birds sang and the clouds disappeared.

4. A young boy ran out on the street his mother ran after him.

5. A young boy ran out on the street and his mother ran after him.

6. A young boy ran out on the street his mother ran after him and caught him by his shirt collar.

7. The café serves delicious pastries and coffee and it is always crowded.

8. The café serves delicious pastries and coffee it is always crowded.

9. The café serves delicious pastries, coffee, and ice cream but it is never crowded.

▶ **Practice 10. Separating independent clauses with periods; connecting them with *and* and *but*.** (Chart 16-4)
Correct the errors in punctuation and capitalization.

(1) My brother is visiting me for a couple of days we spent yesterday together in the city and we had a really good time.

(2) first I took him to the waterfront we went to the aquarium we saw fearsome sharks some wonderfully funny marine mammals and all kinds of tropical fish after the aquarium, we went downtown to a big mall and went shopping.

(3) I had trouble thinking of a place to take him for lunch because he's a strict vegetarian but I remembered a restaurant that has vegan food we went there and we had a wonderful lunch of fresh vegetables and whole grains I'm not a vegetarian but I must say that I really enjoyed the meal.

(4) In the afternoon it started raining we decided to go to a movie it was pretty good but had too much violence for me I felt tense when we left the theater I prefer comedies or dramas my brother loved the movie.

(5) We ended the day with a delicious home-cooked meal and some good conversation in my living room it was an excellent day I like spending time with my brother.

▶ **Practice 11. Chapter review.** (Chapter 16)
Correct the errors. Add the necessary punctuation.

1. Either John will call Mary or Bob.

2. Not only Sue saw the mouse but also the cat.

3. Both my mother talked to the teacher and my father.

4. Either Mr. Anderson or Ms. Wiggins are going to teach our class today.

5. I enjoy not only reading novels but also magazines I enjoy.

6. Smallpox is a dangerous disease. Malaria too. Both are dangerous.

7. She wants to buy a compact car, she is saving her money.

8. According to the news report, it will snow tonight the roads may be dangerous in the morning.

9. While we were in New York, we attended an opera, while we were in New York, we ate at marvelous restaurants, we visited some old friends.

▶ Practice 12. Chapter review.

Complete the crossword puzzle. Use the clues under the puzzle. All the words come from Chapter 16.

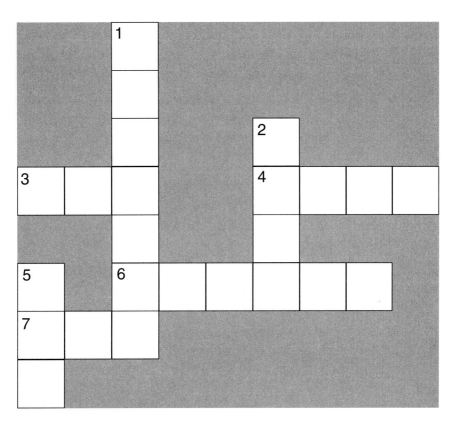

Across

3. I drink tea, _____ I don't drink coffee.
4. Carl is not _____ a chemist but also a biologist.
6. Thankfully, _____ Mary or Joe will help us.
7. He has neither friends _____ money.

Down

1. _____ Jane nor Al speaks Spanish.
2. _____ Sue and Sam are doctors.
5. Salt _____ pepper are on the table.

Chapter 17
Adverb Clauses

▶ **Practice 1. Adverb clauses.** (Chart 17-1)
Underline the adverb clause in each sentence.

1. Sue dropped a carton of eggs <u>as she was leaving the store</u>.

2. Tomorrow, we'll all take a run in the park before we have breakfast.

3. Since Douglas fell off his bicycle last week, he has had to use crutches to walk.

4. Because I already had my boarding pass, I didn't have to stand in line at the airline counter.

5. Productivity in a factory increases if the workplace is made pleasant.

6. After Ceylon had been independent for 24 years, its name was changed to Sri Lanka.

7. Ms. Johnson regularly returns her email messages as soon as she receives them.

8. Tarik will be able to work more efficiently once he becomes familiar with the new computer program.

▶ **Practice 2. Periods and commas.** (Chart 17-1)
Add periods and commas as necessary. Do not change, add, or omit any words. Capitalize as necessary.

1. The lake was calm. Tom went fishing.

2. Because the lake was calm Tom went fishing.

3. Tom went fishing because the lake was calm he caught two fish.

4. When Tom went fishing the lake was calm he caught two fish.

5. The lake was calm so Tom went fishing he caught two fish.

6. Because the lake was calm and quiet Tom went fishing.

7. The lake was calm quiet and clear when Tom went fishing.

8. Because Mr. Hood has dedicated his life to helping the poor he is admired in his community.

9. Mr. Hood is admired because he has dedicated his life to helping the poor he is well known for his work on behalf of homeless people.

10. Microscopes automobile dashboards and cameras are awkward for left-handed people to use they are designed for right-handed people when "lefties" use these items they have to use their right hand to do the things that they would normally do with their left hand.

► **Practice 3. Verb tenses in adverb clauses of time.** (Charts 17-1 and 17-2)
Circle the letter of the correct answer.

1. After Ismael _____ his degree, he plans to seek employment in an engineering firm.
   a. will finish   b. finishes   c. is going to finish   d. is finishing

2. By the time Colette leaves work today, she _____ the budget report.
   a. will finish   b. finishes   c. will have finished   d. had finished

3. When my aunt _____ at the airport tomorrow, I'll be at work, so I can't pick her up.
   a. will arrive   b. arrived   c. will have arrived   d. arrives

4. Natasha heard a small "meow" and looked down to discover a kitten at her feet. When she saw it, she _____.
   a. is smiling   b. had smiled   c. smiled   d. smiles

5. Ahmed has trouble keeping a job. By the time Ahmed was thirty, he _____ eight different jobs.
   a. has   b. was having   c. had had   d. had been having

6. Maria waits until her husband, Al, _____ to work before she calls her friends on the phone.
   a. will go   b. went   c. will have gone   d. goes

7. I went to an opera at Lincoln Center the last time I _____ to New York City.
   a. go   b. went   c. had gone   d. have gone

8. When the police arrived, the building was empty. The thieves _____ and escaped through an unlocked window.
   a. will have   b. have entered   c. had entered   d. were entering

9. It seems that whenever I try to take some quiet time for myself, the phone _____.
   a. has been ringing   b. rings   c. is ringing   d. has rung

10. I'll invite the Thompsons to the potluck dinner the next time I _____ them.
    a. see   b. will see   c. will have seen   d. have seen

11. I _____ hard to help support my family ever since I was a child.
    a. worked   b. work   c. am working   d. have worked

12. A small rabbit ran across the path in front of me as I _____ through the woods.
    a. was walking   b. had walked   c. am walking   d. had been walking

► **Practice 4. Verb tense review.** (Chart 17-2)
Write "1" before the event that happened first. Write "2" before the event that happened second. Write "S" for *same* if the events happened at the same time.

1. As soon as it stopped snowing, the children ran out to go sledding in the fresh snow.

   _1_ It stopped snowing.

   _2_ The children ran out to go sledding.

2. I'll call you as soon as we arrive at the motel.

   ____ I'll call you.

   ____ We arrive at the hotel.

3. We turned on the heat when it got cold.

   ____ It got cold.

   ____ We turned on the heat.

4. We will turn on the heat when it gets cold.

  _____ We will turn on the heat.

  _____ It will get cold.

5. By the time Sharon gets home from Africa, she will have been away for two years.

  _____ Sharon gets home.

  _____ She will have been away.

6. By the time Marc graduated from medical school, he had been studying for 20 years.

  _____ He had been studying.

  _____ Marc graduated from medical school.

7. We were crying while we were watching the movie.

  _____ We were crying.

  _____ We were watching the movie.

8. When I have some news, I'll tell you.

  _____ I have some news.

  _____ I'll tell you.

▶ **Practice 5. Using adverb clauses to show cause and effect.** (Chart 17-3)
Complete the sentences in Column A with a clause from Column B.

Column A

1. I left a message on Jane's voice mail because _____.
2. Since everybody in my office dresses informally, _____.
3. Now that it's summer, _____.
4. I was late for work because _____.
5. Because the temperature dropped below 0 degrees C (32 degrees F), _____.
6. Sue hopes to find a good job now that _____ .
7. I'm not going to the party since _____.
8. We had to eat dinner by candlelight because _____.
9. Since our favorite restaurant was closed, _____.
10. I prefer a small car because _____.

Column B

a. the days are longer
b. we went to another one
c. I wasn't invited
d. she didn't answer her phone
e. the electricity went off
f. there was a big traffic jam
g. it uses less gasoline
h. the water in the lake froze
i. I usually wear jeans to work
j. she has received her master's degree in business

▶ **Practice 6. Using adverb clauses to show cause and effect.** (Chart 17-3)
Combine the sentences. Write one clause in each blank.

1. My registration was canceled. I didn't pay the registration fee on time.

  _____ because _____.

2. I'm late. There was a lot of traffic.

  _____ because _____.

3. Harry lost 35 pounds. He was on a strict weight-loss diet.

  Because _____, _____.

4. We can't have lunch at Mario's tomorrow. It is closed on Sundays.

  Since _____, _____.

5. Jack drives to work. He has a car.

Now that _____ , _____ .

6. Natalie should find another job. She is very unhappy in this job.

_____ since _____ .

7. David knows the way. He will lead us.

_____ because _____ .

8. Frank has graduated from law school. He is looking for a job in a law office.

_____ now that _____ .

▶ **Practice 7. Even though vs. because.** (Charts 17-3 and 17-4)
Circle *even though* or *because*.

1. I put on my raincoat (*even though / because*) it was a bright, sunny day.

2. I put on my raincoat (*even though / because*) it was raining.

3. (*Even though / Because*) Sue is a good student, she received a scholarship.

4. (*Even though / Because*) Ann is a good student, she didn't receive a scholarship.

5. (*Even though / Because*) I was so tired, I didn't want to walk all the way home. I took a taxi.

6. (*Even though / Because*) I was dead tired, I walked all the way home.

7. This letter was delivered (*even though / because*) it didn't have enough postage.

8. That letter was returned to the sender (*even though / because*) it didn't have enough postage.

▶ **Practice 8. Even though vs. because.** (Charts 17-3 and 17-4)
Complete the sentences with *even though* or *because*.

1. I'm going horseback riding with Judy this afternoon _____ I'm afraid of horses.

2. I'm going horseback riding with Judy this afternoon _____ I enjoy it.

3. _____ the economy is not good right now, people are not buying new cars and other expensive items.

4. _____ the economy is not good right now, the supermarket is still a profitable business. People always have to eat.

5. Members of the Polar Bear Club are swimmers who go swimming in the ocean _____ the temperature may be freezing.

6. Members of the Polar Bear Club are swimmers who swim in the ocean every day in summer and winter _____ they love to swim in the ocean.

7. Janet got a grade of 98 percent on her history test _____ she studied hard.

8. Mike got a grade of 98 percent on his history test _____ he didn't study at all. I wonder how that happened.

► **Practice 9. Showing direct contrast: *while*.** (Chart 17-5)
Circle the letter of the phrase that shows direct contrast.

1. Larry and Barry are twins, but they are very different. Larry never studies, while Barry _____.
    a. rarely studies
    b. sleeps all day
    c. is very studious

2. My roommate and I disagree about the room temperature. While she likes it warm, I _____.
    a. prefer cold temperatures
    b. have trouble when it is cool
    c. don't like my roommate

3. Athletes need to be strong, but they may need different physical characteristics for different sports. For example, weight-lifters have well-developed chest muscles, while _____.
    a. basketball players' muscles are strong
    b. basketball players should be tall
    c. basketball players' chest muscles are very large

4. Portland, Maine, is on the East Coast of the United States, while Portland, Oregon, _____.
    a. is on the East Coast too
    b. lies on the West Coast
    c. is another medium-sized city

5. Crocodiles and alligators look a lot alike, but they have certain differences. While a crocodile has a very long, narrow, V-shaped snout, the alligator's snout is _____.
    a. wider and U-shaped
    b. long, narrow, and V-shaped
    c. large and green

6. The Earth is similar to Venus in some ways, but their atmospheres are different. While the Earth's atmosphere contains mostly nitrogen and oxygen, _____.
    a. Venus has mainly nitrogen and oxygen
    b. Venus' air is very cold
    c. Venus' atmosphere consists mostly of the gas carbon dioxide

7. Polar bears live near the North Pole, while _____.
    a. penguins live there too
    b. penguins live at the South Pole
    c. they live in the South Pole

8. Potatoes and tomatoes originated in the Americas, while _____.
    a. mangos and bananas come from Asia
    b. corn and chocolate come from the Americas
    c. turkeys first lived in North America

► **Practice 10. *If*-clauses.** (Chart 17-6)
Underline the entire *if*-clause. Correct any errors in verb forms. Some sentences have no errors.

                     rains
1. We won't go to the beach if it ~~will rain~~ tomorrow.

2. If my car doesn't start tomorrow morning, I'll take the bus to work. (*no change*)

3. If I have any free time during my work day, I'll call you.

4. I'll send you an email if I will have some free time tomorrow.

5. If we don't leave within the next ten minutes, we are late for the theater.

6. If we will leave within the next ten minutes, we will make it to the theater on time.

7. The population of the world will be 9.1 billion in 2050 if it will continue to grow at the present

    rate.

► **Practice 11. Shortened *if*-clauses.** (Chart 17-7)
First, complete the sentences in two ways:
    a. Use *so* or *not*.
    b. Use a helping verb or main verb *be*.
Then, give the full meaning of the shortened *if*-clause.

1. Does Tom live near you?
    a. If _____*so*_____, ask him to pick you up at 5:30.
    b. If he _____*does*_____, ask him to pick you up at 5:30.
    Meaning: _____*If Tom lives near you*_____

2. Are you a resident of Springfield?
    a. If _____, you can get a library card for the Springfield Library.
    b. If you _____, you can get a library card for the Springfield Library.
    Meaning: _____

3. Do you have enough money to go out to dinner?
    a. If _____, I'll pay for you.
    b. If you _____, I'll pay for you.
    Meaning: _____

4. Are you going to do the laundry?
    a. If _____, I have some things that need washing too.
    b. If you _____, I have some things that need washing too.
    Meaning: _____

5. I think I left the water running in the sink.
    a. If _____, we'd better go home and turn it off.
    b. If I _____, we'd better go home and turn it off.
    Meaning: _____

▶ **Practice 12. Using *whether or not* and *even if.*** (Chart 17-8)
Complete the sentences using the given information.

1. Juan is going to go to the horse races no matter what. He doesn't care if his wife approves. In other words, Juan is going to go to the horse races even if his wife _____doesn't approve_____. He's going to go whether his wife _____approves_____ or not.

2. Fatima is determined to buy an expensive car. It doesn't matter to her if she can't afford it. In other words, Fatima is going to buy an expensive car whether she _____ it or not. She's going to buy one even if she _____ it.

3. William wears his raincoat every day. He wears it when it's raining. He wears it when it's not raining. In other words, William wears his raincoat whether it _____ or not. He wears it even if it _____.

4. Some students don't understand what the teacher is saying, but still they smile and nod. In other words, even if they _____ what the teacher is saying, they smile and nod. They smile and nod whether they _____ what the teacher is saying or not.

5. Everybody has to pay taxes. It doesn't matter whether you want to or not. In other words, even if you _____ , you have to pay them. You have to pay your taxes _____ or not.

▶ **Practice 13. Adverb clauses of condition: using *unless.*** (Chart 17-10)
The sentences in *italics* are well-known proverbs or sayings. Write sentences with the same meaning as the sentences in *italics*. Use ***unless***.

1. *If you can't stand the heat, get out of the kitchen.*
    (This means that if you can't take the pressure, then you should remove yourself from the situation.)
    Get out of the kitchen _____unless you can stand the heat_____.

2. *If it isn't broken, don't fix it.* (This is often said as *If it ain't broke, don't fix it.*)
    (This means that any attempt to improve something that already works is pointless and may even hurt it.)
    Don't fix it _____.

3. *If you can't beat 'em, join 'em.*
    (This means if you can't beat your opponents, you can join them.)
    You might not be successful _____.

▶ **Practice 14. Adverb clauses of condition: using _only if._** (Chart 17-11)
Complete the sentences with the information in the given sentence.

1. Jack never calls his uncle unless he wants something.

   Jack calls his uncle only if _____.

2. When Helen runs out of clean clothes, she does her laundry. Otherwise, she never does

   laundry.

   Helen does laundry only if _____.

3. José doesn't like to turn on the heat in his house unless the temperature outside goes below 50

   degrees F (10 degrees C).

   José turns on the heat only if _____.

4. Zack hates to fly. He usually travels by car or train except when it is absolutely necessary to

   get somewhere quickly.

   Zack flies only if _____.

5. Most applicants cannot get into Halley College. You probably won't get in. Only the top

   students will get in.

   Only if you are a top student _____.

6. I could never afford a big house like that! Well, maybe if I win the lottery. That would be the

   only way.

   Only if I win the lottery _____.

▶ **Practice 15. Review: adverb clauses of condition.** (Charts 17-8 → 17-11)
Circle the correct words in parentheses to logically complete each sentence.

1. I'll pass the course only if I (_pass / don't pass_) the final examination.

2. I'm (_going to go / not going to go_) to the park unless the weather is nice.

3. I'm going to the park unless it (_rains / doesn't rain_).

4. I'm sorry that you won't join us on Saturday. But please call us (_in case / even if_) you change

   your mind.

5. Bob doesn't like to work. He'll get a job (_unless / only if_) he has to.

6. I (_always eat / never eat_) breakfast unless I get up late and don't have enough time.

7. I always finish my homework (_even if / only if_) I'm sleepy and want to go to bed.

8. Ali is at his desk at 8:00 A.M. sharp (_whether / unless_) his boss is there or not.

9. You (_will / won't_) learn to play the guitar well unless you practice every day.

10. Even if the president calls, (_wake / don't wake_) me up. I don't want to talk to anyone. I need

    to sleep.

11. Burt is going to come to the game with us today (_if / unless_) his boss gives him the afternoon

    off.

12. Only if people succeed in reducing greenhouse gases (_we can / can we_) avoid the effects of

    global warming.

▶ **Practice 16. Adverb clauses.** (Chapter 17)
Complete the sentences with the correct phrase from the list. Write the letter of the phrase.

a. her friend goes with her
b. I don't eat meat
c. I don't have an 8:00 A.M. class anymore
d. I eat meat

e. I'm working on the weekends now
f. none of her friends will go with her
g. you have a real emergency
h. you promise to keep it a secret

1. A: Won't you tell me about Emma and Tom? Oh, please tell me!

   B: Well, OK, I'll tell you, but only if _____.

2. A: Hello, 911? Police? I want to report a barking dog.

   B: This is 911. You've dialed the wrong number. Call this number only in case _____.

3. A: Isn't Sara coming to the party?

   B: I don't think so. She's too shy to come alone. She doesn't go anyplace unless _____.

4. A: Your grandmother has traveled to 32 countries all by herself?

   B: Yes, she has! She loves to travel to exotic places even if _____.

5. A: Do you want to go to Johnson's Steak House or Vernon's Vegetable Stand for lunch?

   B: Definitely, Vernon's Vegetable Stand since _____.

6. A: They say that people who don't eat meat live longer than people who do.

   B: Well, I think that I will live a certain number of years whether or not _____.

7. A: You haven't come to our book club for months! How come?

   B: Oh, I can't come on Saturdays anymore because _____.

8. A: Hi, Kevin. . . . Oh, did I wake you up? It's 7:30 already! You need to get up.

   B: I sleep later now, Andy, since _____.

▶ **Practice 17. Chapter review.**
Circle the letter of the adverb or adverb phrase that best completes each sentence.

1. Alice will tutor you in math _____ you promise to show up promptly every day.
   a. unless   b. only if   c. whereas   d. even though

2. Oscar won't pass his math course _____ he gets a tutor.
   a. in case   b. unless   c. only if   d. because

3. Most people you meet will be polite to you _____ you are polite to them.
   a. in case   b. even though   c. unless   d. if

4. I'm glad that my mother made me take piano lessons when I was a child _____ I hated it at the time. Now, I enjoy playing the piano every day.
   a. even though   b. because   c. unless   d. if

5. Chicken eggs will not hatch _____ they are kept at the proper temperature.
   a. because   b. unless   c. only if   d. even though

6. You'd better take your raincoat with you _____ the weather changes. It could rain before you get home again.
    a. now that   b. even if   c. in case   d. only if

7. Ms. Jackson was assigned the fifth-grade science class _____ she has the best science qualifications of all the teachers in that elementary school.
    a. although   b. whereas   c. if   d. since

8. My sister can fall asleep under any conditions, but I can't get to sleep _____ the light is off and the room is perfectly quiet.
    a. if   b. unless   c. in case   d. now that

9. In a democratic government, a leader is directly responsible to the people, _____ in a dictatorship, a leader has no direct responsibility to the people.
    a. because   b. even though   c. while   d. unless

10. Parents love and support their children _____ the children misbehave or do foolish things.
    a. even if   b. since   c. if   d. only if

Chapter 18
Reduction of Adverb Clauses to Modifying Adverbial Phrases

▶ **Practice 1. Introduction.** (Chart 18-1)
Each sentence contains either an adverb clause or an adverb phrase. <u>Underline</u> the adverb clause or phrase in each sentence.

1. <u>While they were riding in the car for six hours</u>, the children became restless.

2. <u>While riding in the car for six hours</u>, the children became restless.

3. Before taking our long car trip across the country, we had drawn our route on a large road map.

4. While watching the exciting basketball game on TV, the boys forgot all about dinner.

5. While they were watching the exciting basketball game on TV, the boys forgot all about dinner.

6. Before leaving for the airport, we checked to make sure we had all our travel necessities with us.

7. We heard a lot of thunder while we were walking on the beach this afternoon.

8. We heard a lot of thunder while walking on the beach this afternoon.

9. While I was trying to get a taxi, I was almost run over by several taxis that

   passed me by.

10. Before getting into a taxi, I was almost run over by several that passed me by.

▶ **Practice 2. Modifying adverbial phrases.** (Chart 18-2)
Check the grammatically correct sentences.

1. ___ While watching an exciting program, the TV suddenly went off.
2. ___ While starting up, my computer suddenly crashed.
3. ___ While watching an exciting program, I fell asleep.
4. ___ Before going to bed, I always open the bedroom windows.
5. ___ Before going to bed, the bedroom windows are always open.
6. ___ After opening the bedroom windows, I crawl into bed for the night.
7. ___ Since graduating from college, nobody has offered me a job yet.
8. ___ Since graduating from college, I haven't found a job yet.
9. ___ After sitting on her eggs for four weeks, we saw the mother duck welcome her baby ducklings.
10. ___ After sitting on her eggs for four weeks, the mother duck welcomed her baby ducklings.

▶ **Practice 3. Changing time clauses to modifying adverbial phrases.**
(Chart 18-2)
Change the adverb clause to a modifying phrase.

        opening
1. Since ~~he opened~~ his new business, Bob has been working sixteen hours a day.

2. I shut off the lights before I left the room.

3. After I had met the movie star in person, I understood why she was so popular.

4. After I searched through all my pockets, I found my keys.

5. While he was herding his goats in the mountains, an Ethiopian named Kaldi discovered the coffee plant more than 1,200 years ago.

6. Before they marched into battle, ancient Ethiopian soldiers ate a mixture of coffee beans and fat for extra energy.

7. While she was flying across the Pacific Ocean in 1937, the famous pilot Amelia Earhart disappeared.

8. After they imported rabbits to Australia, the settlers found that these animals became pests.

▶ **Practice 4. Adverb clauses and modifying phrases.** (Charts 18-1 → 18-3)
Complete the sentences with the correct form of the verb in parentheses.

1. a. Before (leave) _____*leaving*_____ on his trip, Tom renewed his passport.
   b. Before Tom (leave) _____*left*_____ on his trip, he renewed his passport.

2. a. After Thomas Edison (invent) _____*invented / had invented*_____ the light bulb, he went on to create many other useful inventions.
   b. After (invent) _____*inventing / having invented*_____ the light bulb, Thomas Edison went on to create many other useful inventions.

3. a. While (work) _____ with uranium ore, Marie Curie discovered two new elements, radium and polonium.
   b. While she (work) _____ with uranium ore, Marie Curie discovered two new elements, radium and polonium.

4. a. Before an astronaut (fly) _____ on a space mission, she will have undergone thousands of hours of training.
   b. Before (fly) _____ on a space mission, an astronaut will have undergone thousands of hours of training.

5. a. After they (study) _____ the stars, the ancient Mayans in Central America developed a very accurate solar calendar.
   b. After (study) _____ the stars, the ancient Mayans in Central America developed a very accurate solar calendar.

6. a. Since (learn) _____ that cigarettes cause cancer, many people have stopped smoking.

   b. Since they (learn) _____ that cigarettes cause cancer, many people have stopped smoking.

7. a. When (take) _____ any medication, you should be sure to follow the directions on the label.

   b. When you (take) _____ any medication, you should be sure to follow the directions on the label.

8. a. While I (drive) _____ to my uncle's house, I took a wrong turn and ended up back where I had started.

   b. While (drive) _____ to my uncle's house, I took a wrong turn and ended up back where I had started.

▶ **Practice 5. Expressing the idea of "during the same time" in modifying adverbial phrases.** (Chart 18-3)

<u>Underline</u> the subject of the adverb clause and the subject of the main clause. Change the adverb clauses to modifying phrases if possible.

1. While <u>Sam</u> was driving to work in the rain, his <u>car</u> got a flat tire.

   _(no change)_____

2. While <u>Sam</u> was driving to work, <u>he</u> had a flat tire.

   _While driving to work, Sam had a flat tire._____

3. Before Nick left on his trip, his son gave him a big hug and a kiss.

   _____

4. Before Nick left on his trip, he gave his itinerary to his secretary.

   _____

5. After Tom had worked hard in the garden all afternoon, he took a shower and then went to the movies with his friends.

   _____

6. After Sunita had made a delicious chicken curry for her friends, they wanted the recipe.

   _____

7. Before a friend tries to do something hard, an American may say "Break a leg!" to wish him or her good luck.

   _____

8. Emily always cleans off her desk before she leaves the office at the end of each day.

   _____

▶ Practice 6. Expressing the idea of "during the same time" and cause/effect in modifying adverbial phrases. (Charts 18-3 and 18-4)

<u>Underline</u> the modifying adverbial phrase in each sentence. Then circle the letter of the meaning of each modifying phrase. In some sentences, both meanings may be given.

1. Riding his bicycle to school, Enrique fell off and scraped his knee.
   a. while   b. because

2. Being seven feet tall, the basketball player couldn't sit in a regular airplane seat.
   a. while   b. because

3. Driving to work this morning, I remembered that I had already missed the special 8:00 A.M. breakfast meeting.
   a. while   b. because

4. Running five miles on a very hot day, James felt exhausted.
   a. while   b. because

5. Having run for 26 miles in the marathon, the runners were exhausted at the end of the race.
   a. while   b. because

6. Drinking a tall glass of soothing iced tea, Ann felt her tired muscles relax.
   a. while   b. because

7. Clapping loudly at the end of the game, the fans showed their appreciation of the team.
   a. while   b. because

8. Speaking with her guidance counselor, Carol felt that she was being understood.
   a. while   b. because

9. Knowing that I was going to miss the plane because of heavy traffic, I phoned the airline to get a seat on a later plane.
   a. while   b. because

10. Having missed my plane, I had to wait four hours to take the next one.
    a. while   b. because

11. Waiting for my plane to depart, I watched thousands of people walking through the airport.
    a. while   b. because

▶ Practice 7. Expressing the idea of "during the same time" and cause/effect in modifying adverbial phrases. (Charts 18-3 and 18-4)

Complete the sentences in Column A with a clause from Column B.

Column A

1. Talking on the phone with my friend, _____.
2. While watching an old movie on TV _____.
3. Drinking a big glass of water in four seconds, _____.
4. Because I like old movies, _____.
5. Since receiving a big job promotion, _____.
6. Having finished my long report, _____.
7. Unable to reach my friend by phone, _____.
8. Being a shy person, _____.
9. Having lived in Rome for two years, _____.
10. Wanting to get home quickly, _____.

Column B

a. I handed it in to my supervisor this morning
b. I watch a lot of them on TV late at night
c. I decided to email her
d. I have more responsibility
e. I can speak Italian
f. I don't like to go to parties alone
g. I ran all the way
h. I heard the click of the phone disconnecting
i. I fell asleep
j. I quenched my thirst

▶ Practice 8. Modifying phrases and clauses. (Charts 18-2 →18-4)

Circle all the possible completions for each sentence. More than one may be correct.

1. Before _____ you, I had not known such a wonderful person existed!
   a. met   b. meeting   c. I met

2. After _____ what the candidate had to say, I am considering voting for him.
   a. I heard   b. having heard   c. hearing

3. Since _____ married, Fred seems very happy and content.
   a. he got   b. getting   c. got

4. _____ through outer space at a speed of 25,000 miles per hour (40,000 kilometers), the astronauts were able to see the Earth.
   a. Speeding   b. While speeding   c. Sped

5. _____ president of his new country, George Washington had been a general in its army.
   a. Before becoming   b. While becoming   c. Before he became

6. _____ rap music before, our grandparents wondered why it was so popular.
   a. Had never heard   b. Because they had never heard   c. Never having heard

7. _____ the English faculty, Professor Wilson has become the most popular teacher at our university.
   a. Since joining   b. While joining   c. Since he joined

▶ **Practice 9. Modifying phrases with _upon._** (Chart 18-5)
Rewrite the sentences with the given words.

1. When Sarah received her acceptance letter for medical school, she shouted for joy.

   a. Upon _____.

   b. On _____.

2. On hearing the sad news, Kathleen began to cry.

   a. Upon _____.

   b. When _____.

3. Upon looking at the accident victim, the paramedics decided to transport him to the hospital.

   a. On _____.

   b. When _____.

▶ **Practice 10. Modifying phrases with _upon._** (Chart 18-5)
Complete the sentences using the ideas in the given list.

    a. She learned the problem was not at all serious.
    b. She was told she got it.
    c. She discovered a burnt-out wire.
   ✓d. She arrived at the airport.
    e. She reached the other side of the lake.

1. It had been a long, uncomfortable trip. Upon _____<u>arriving at the airport</u>_____, Sue
   quickly unfastened her seat belt and stood in the aisle waiting her turn to disembark.

2. Kim rented a small fishing boat last weekend, but she ended up doing more rowing than
   fishing. The motor died halfway across the lake, so she had to row to shore. It was a long
   distance away. Upon _____, she was exhausted.

3. At first, we thought the fire had been caused by lightning. However, upon
   _____, the fire chief determined it had been
   caused by faulty electrical wiring.

4. Amy felt terrible. She was sure she had some terrible disease, so she went to the doctor for
   some tests. Upon _____, she was extremely
   relieved.

5. Janet wanted that scholarship with all her heart and soul. Upon _____
   _____, she jumped straight up in the air and let out a scream of
   happiness.

► **Practice 11. Modifying phrases.** (Charts 18-1 → 18-5)
Write the letter of a clause from the list that logically follows the modifying phrase.

a. the desperate woman grasped a floating log after the boat turned over
b. the taxi driver caused a multiple-car accident
c. carefully proofread all your answers
d. the students repeated the experiment
e. the athletes waved to the cheering crowd
f. the little girl raised her hand

g. the manager learned of their dissatisfaction with their jobs
h. the passengers angrily walked back to the ticket counter
i. Margo hasn't been able to play tennis
j. the worker in charge of Section B of the assembly line told the assistant manager about a production problem

1. Trying to understand the physics problem, _____.

2. Fighting for her life, _____.

3. Wanting to ask a question, _____.

4. After having injured her ankle, _____.

5. Not wanting to disturb the manager, _____.

6. Upon hearing the announcement that their plane was delayed, _____.

7. Talking with the employees after work, _____.

8. Attempting to get onto the freeway, _____.

9. Stepping onto the platform to receive their medals, _____.

10. Before turning in your exam paper, _____.

Chapter 19

Connectives That Express Cause and Effect, Contrast, and Condition

▶ **Practice 1. Using *because of* and *due to*.** (Chart 19-1)
Circle the letters of the words that can complete each sentence. More than one answer is possible.

1. The plane was delayed because _____.
   a. bad weather
   b. the weather was bad
   c. there was heavy air traffic
   d. heavy air traffic
   e. mechanical difficulty
   f. the mechanics had to make a repair

2. The plane was delayed because of _____.
   a. bad weather
   b. the weather was bad
   c. there was heavy air traffic
   d. heavy air traffic
   e. mechanical difficulty
   f. the mechanics had to make a repair

3. The thief was caught because _____.
   a. the police responded quickly
   b. the quick police response
   c. he left fingerprints
   d. the fingerprints on the door
   e. there was a security video
   f. a security video

4. The thief was caught due to _____.
   a. the police responded quickly
   b. the quick police response
   c. he left fingerprints
   d. the fingerprints on the door
   e. there was a security video
   f. a security video

▶ **Practice 2. Using *because of* and *due to*.** (Chart 19-1)
Circle the words or phrases that can complete the sentences correctly. In some sentences, more than one completion is correct.

1. We delayed our trip (*because* / *because of* / *due to*) Dad was sick with the flu.

2. Sue's eyes were red (*due to* / *because of* / *because*) she had been crying.

3. The water in most rivers is unsafe to drink (*because* / *due to* / *because of*) pollution.

4. The water in most rivers is unsafe to drink (*because* / *due to* / *because of*) it is polluted.

5. Some people think Harry succeeded in business (*due to* / *because of* / *because*) his charming personality rather than his business skills.

6. You can't enter this secured area (*because of* / *because* / *due to*) you don't have an official permit.

7. My lecture notes were incomplete (*due to* / *because of* / *because*) the instructor talked too fast.

8. It's unsafe to travel in that country (*because* / *due to* / *because of*) the ongoing civil war.

▶ **Practice 3. Using *because of* and *due to*.** (Chart 19-1)
Use the ideas in parentheses to complete the sentences.

1. (*There was heavy traffic.*) We were late due to _____heavy traffic_____.

2. (*There was heavy traffic.*) We were late because _____.

3. (*Grandpa is getting old.*) Grandpa doesn't like to drive at night anymore because

   _____.

4. (*Our history professor is quite old.*) Our history professor is going to retire because of

   _____.

5. (*Sarah is afraid of heights.*) She will not walk across a bridge because

   _____.

6. (*Sarah is afraid of heights.*) She will not walk across a bridge because of

   _____.

7. (*There was a cancellation.*) Due to _____, you can

   have an appointment with the doctor this afternoon.

8. (*There was a cancellation today.*) Because _____, you

   can have an appointment with the doctor this afternoon.

▶ **Practice 4. Cause and effect: using *therefore*, *consequently*, and *so*.**
   (Chart 19-2)
Punctuate the sentences in Column B. Add capital letters if necessary.

Column A	Column B
1. *adverb clause:*	Because she had a headache she took some aspirin.
2. *adverb clause:*	She took some aspirin because she had a headache.
3. *prepositional phrase:*	Because of her headache she took some aspirin.
4. *prepositional phrase:*	She took some aspirin because of her headache.
5. *transition:*	She had a headache therefore she took some aspirin.
6. *transition:*	She had a headache she therefore took some aspirin.
7. *transition:*	She had a headache she took some aspirin therefore.
8. *conjunction:*	She had a headache so she took some aspirin.

▶ **Practice 5. Cause and effect: using *therefore*, *consequently*, and *so*.**
   (Chart 19-2)
Each sentence in *italics* is followed by sentences that refer to it. Circle the letter of the word that logically completes each sentence. Notice the punctuation and capitalization.

SENTENCE 1. *Water boils when its temperature reaches 212 degrees Fahrenheit* (100 degrees Celsius).

1. The water in the pot had reached 212 degrees Fahrenheit. _____, it started to boil.
   (a.) Therefore   b. So   c. Because

2. The water in the pot started to boil _____ it had reached 212 degrees Fahrenheit.
   a. so   b. because   c. therefore

3. The water in the pot had reached 212 degrees Fahrenheit, _____ it started to boil.
    a. because   b. therefore   c. so

SENTENCE 2. *The main highway is closed.*

1. The main highway is closed. _____ , we are going to take another road.
    a. Therefore   b. Because   c. so

2. We are going to take another road _____ the main highway is closed.
    a. so   b. because   c. therefore

3. The main highway is closed. We are going to take another road, _____.
    a. therefore   b. Therefore   c. so

4. The main highway is closed, _____ we are going to take another road.
    a. So   b. so   c. therefore

▶ **Practice 6. Cause and effect: using *therefore, consequently*, and *so*.**
        (Chart 19-2)

Combine the two sentences in *italics* in four different ways. Notice the punctuation and capitalization.

1. *The store didn't have orange juice. I bought lemonade instead.*

    a. _____I bought lemonade_____ because the store _____didn't have any orange juice_____ .

    b. Because _____ , _____ .

    c. _____ . Therefore, _____

    _____ .

    d. _____ , so _____ .

2. *Mel has excellent grades. He will go to a top university.*

    a. _____ . Therefore, _____ .

    b. _____ . He, therefore, _____ .

    c. _____ . _____ , therefore.

    d. _____ , so _____ .

3. *There had been no rain for several months. The crops died.*

    a. Because _____ , _____ .

    b. _____ . Consequently, _____ .

    c. _____ . _____ , therefore,

    _____ .

    d. _____ , so _____ .

► **Practice 7. Showing cause and effect.** (Charts 17-3, 19-1, and 19-2)

Part I. Complete the sentences with *because of*, *because*, or *therefore*. Add any necessary punctuation and capitalization.

1. _____*Because*_____ it rained **,** we stayed home.

2. It rained. _____*Therefore*_____ **,** we stayed home.

3. We stayed home _____*because of*_____ the bad weather.

4. The weather was bad. _____ we stayed home.

5. The typhoon was moving directly toward a small coastal town. _____ all residents were advised to move inland until it passed.

6. The residents moved inland _____ the typhoon.

7. _____ the typhoon was moving directly toward the town all residents were advised to move inland.

8. Giraffes, which are found in the African plains, are the tallest of all animals. Although their bodies are not extremely large, they have very long necks. _____ their long necks, they are tall enough to eat the leaves from the tops of the trees.

Part II. Complete the sentence with *due to*, *since*, or *consequently*. Add any necessary punctuation and capitalization.

9. _____ his poor eyesight John has to sit in the front row in class.

10. _____ John has poor eyesight he has to sit in the front row.

11. John has poor eyesight _____ he has to sit in the front row.

12. Sarah is afraid of heights _____ she will not walk across a bridge.

13. Sarah will not walk across a bridge _____ her fear of heights.

14. Mark is overweight _____ his doctor has advised him to exercise regularly.

15. _____ a diamond is extremely hard, it can be used to cut glass.

► **Practice 8. Periods and commas.** (Chart 19-3)
Punctuate the sentences properly, using periods and commas. Add capital letters if necessary.

1. Edward missed the final exam. ~~t~~^Therefore **,** he failed the course.

2. Edward failed the course because he missed the final exam. (*no change*)

3. Edward missed the final exam **.** ~~h~~^He simply forgot to go to it.

4. Because we forgot to make a reservation we couldn't get a table at our favorite restaurant last night.

5. The waitress kept dropping trays full of dishes therefore she was fired.

6. The waiter kept forgetting customers' orders so he was fired.

7. Ron is an unpleasant dinner companion because of his terrible table manners.

8. The needle has been around since prehistoric times the button was invented about 2,000 years ago the zipper wasn't invented until 1890.

9. It is possible for wildlife observers to identify individual zebras because the patterns of stripes on each zebra are unique no two zebras are alike.

10. When students in the United States are learning to type, they often practice this sentence: *The quick brown fox jumps over the lazy dog* because it contains all the letters of the English alphabet.

▶ **Practice 9. Summary of patterns and punctuation.** (Chart 19-3)
Combine the two sentences in *italics*. Use the words in parentheses in the new sentences.

SENTENCE 1. *Kim ate some bad food. She got sick.*

a. *(because)* _____

b. *(because of)* _____

c. *(so)* _____

d. *(due to)* _____

SENTENCE 2. *Adam was exhausted. He had driven for thirteen hours.*

a. *(therefore)* _____

b. *(since)* _____

c. *(due to the fact that)* _____

d. *(so)* _____

▶ **Practice 10. *Such . . . that* and *so . . . that*.** (Chart 19-4)
Write **such** or **so** to complete the sentences.

1. It was ____such____ a hot day that we canceled our tennis game.

2. The test was ____so____ easy that everyone got a high score.

3. The movie was _____ bad that we left early.

4. It was _____ a bad movie that we left early.

5. Professor James is _____ a demanding teacher that many students refuse to take his class.

6. The restaurant patron at the table near us was _____ angry that we became very frightened and left our meals unfinished.

7. The intricate metal lacework on the Eiffel Tower in Paris was _____ complicated that the structure took more than two and a half years to complete.

8. Charles and his brother are _____ hard-working carpenters that I'm sure they'll make a success of their new business.

9. The children had _____ much fun at the carnival that they begged to go again.

10. I feel like I have _____ little energy that I wonder if I'm getting sick.

▶ **Practice 11. Such...that and so...that.** (Chart 19-4)
Combine the two sentences. Use *so ... that* or *such ... that*.

1. We took a walk. It was a nice day.

    It was _____ such a nice day that we took a walk _____ .

2. The weather was hot. You could fry an egg on the sidewalk.

    The weather _____ .

3. I couldn't understand her. She talked too fast.

    She talked _____ .

4. It was an expensive car. We couldn't afford to buy it.

    It was _____ .

5. There were few people at the meeting. It was canceled.

    There were _____ .

6. Ted couldn't fall asleep last night. He was worried about the exam.

    Ted was _____ .

7. The tornado struck with great force. It lifted automobiles off the ground.

    The tornado _____ .

8. I can't figure out what this sentence says. Joe's handwriting is illegible.

    Joe's handwriting _____ .

9. David has too many girlfriends. He can't remember all of their names.

    David has _____ .

10. Too many people came to the meeting. There were not enough seats for everyone.

    There were _____ .

▶ **Practice 12. Expressing purpose.** (Chart 19-5)
Check the sentences that express purpose.

1. _____ Ali changed jobs in order to be closer to his family.

2. _____ Ali changed jobs, so he has a lot of new information to learn.

3. _____ Ali changed jobs so he could be involved in more interesting work.

4. _____ Ali changed jobs so that he could be closer to his family.

5. _____ The highway will be closed tomorrow so that road crews can make repairs to the road.

6. _____ The highway will be closed tomorrow, so you will need to take a detour.

7. _____ The highway will be closed tomorrow so the road can be repaired.

8. _____ The highway will be closed tomorrow in order for road crews to make repairs.

9. _____ The highway will be closed tomorrow, so we can expect long delays.

10. _____ The highway will be closed tomorrow, so let's do our errands today.

► **Practice 13. Expressing purpose: using *so that.*** (Chart 19-5)
Complete the sentences in Column A with a clause from Column B.

Column A

1. Please open the windows so that _____.
2. Sam put on his boots so that _____.
3. I spoke softly on the phone so that _____.
4. Li bought a very small car so that _____.
5. Fred stayed up all night so that _____.
6. You could lower the price on the house you are trying to sell so that _____.
7. The city has put up a traffic light at the busy intersection so that _____.
8. We are painting the kitchen yellow so that _____.
9. Sid wore a suit and tie for his interview so that _____.
10. Mr. Kim studies advanced Russian so that _____.

Column B

a. my roommate wouldn't wake up
b. he can be a translator
c. it can sell more quickly
d. we can have some fresh air
e. it will be safer for drivers and pedestrians
f. he will be able to save money on gasoline
g. it will look bright and cheerful
h. he would look serious and businesslike
i. he could go hiking in the mountains
j. he could finish writing his long report by morning

► **Practice 14. Using modals with *so that.*** (Chart 19-5)
Decide the meaning of the *so that* clause. Write "1" if the modal verb expresses the idea of *to be able to.* Write "2" if the modal verb expresses the idea of *to make sure.*

1 = to be able to   2 = to make sure

1. _____ The hotel manager asked a guest to turn down her music so that other guests could sleep.
2. _____ Ellen looks for airline tickets online so that she can compare prices.
3. _____ Yoshi arrived at the theater early so that he could get a good seat.
4. _____ Yoshi arrived at the theater early so that he would get a good seat.
5. _____ I'll send your package express mail so that you'll get it the day after tomorrow.
6. _____ I left your dinner in the oven so that it would stay warm.
7. _____ Karin changes her bank password regularly so that no one can access her account.
8. _____ John, you overslept, but I'll drive you to work so that you won't be late.

► **Practice 15. Expressing purpose: using *so that.*** (Chart 19-5)
Write a sentence with the same meaning. Use *so that.*

1. Rachel wanted to watch the news. She turned on the TV.
   Rachel turned on the TV so that she could watch the news.

2. Alex wrote down the time and date of his appointment. He didn't want to forget to go.
   Alex wrote down the time and date of his appointment so that he wouldn't forget to go.

3. Nancy is taking extra courses every semester. She wants to graduate early.
   _____

4. Sue didn't want to disturb her roommate. She lowered the volume on the TV set.
   _____

5. Ed took some change from his pocket. He wanted to buy a newspaper.

_____

6. I wanted to listen to the news while I was making dinner. I turned on the TV.

_____

7. I turned off my phone. I didn't want to be interrupted while I was working.

_____

8. It's a good idea for you to learn keyboarding skills. You'll be able to use your computer more

efficiently. _____

_____

9. Lynn wanted to make sure that she didn't forget to take her book back to the library. She tied

a string around her finger. _____

_____

10. The Parks Department has placed wastebaskets in convenient places in the park. The

department wants to make sure people don't litter.

_____

_____

▶ **Practice 16. Showing contrast (unexpected result).** (Chart 19-6)
Make logical completions by completing the sentences with *is* or *isn't*.

1. It's the middle of the summer, but the weather _____ very cold.
2. It's the middle of the summer; nevertheless, the weather _____ very cold.
3. The weather _____ warm today even though it's the middle of summer.
4. Although it's the middle of the summer, the weather _____ very cold today.
5. Even though it's the middle of summer, the weather _____ very cold today.
6. It's the middle of summer in spite of the fact that the weather _____ very warm today.
7. Despite the fact that it is the middle of summer, the weather _____ very cold today.
8. It's the middle of summer. However, the weather _____ warm today.
9. It's the middle of summer, yet the weather _____ very warm today.
10. Despite the cold weather, it _____ the middle of summer.

▶ **Practice 17. *Despite, in spite of* vs. *even though, although*.** (Chart 19-6)
Circle the word or phrase to complete the sentence correctly.

1. a. (*Even though* / *Despite*) her doctor has prescribed frequent exercise for her, Carol never
   does any exercise at all.

   b. (*Even though* / *Despite*) her doctor's orders, Carol has not done any exercise at all.

   c. (*Even though* / *Despite*) the orders her doctor gave her, Carol still hasn't done any exercise.

   d. (*Even though* / *Despite*) the dangers of not exercising, Carol still doesn't exercise.

   e. (*Even though* / *Despite*) she has been warned about the dangers of not exercising by her
   doctor, Carol still hasn't begun to exercise.

2. a. (*Although* / *In spite of*) an approaching storm, the two climbers continued their trek up the mountain.

   b. (*Although* / *In spite of*) a storm was approaching, the two climbers continued their trek.

   c. (*Although* / *In spite of*) there was an approaching storm, the two climbers continued up the mountain.

   d. (*Although* / *In spite of*) the storm that was approaching the mountain area, the two climbers continued their trek.

   e. (*Although* / *In spite of*) the fact that a storm was approaching the mountain area, the two climbers continued their trek.

3. a. (*Although* / *Despite*) his many hours of practice, George failed his driving test for the third time.

   b. (*Although* / *Despite*) he had practiced for many hours, George failed his driving test for the third time.

   c. (*Although* / *Despite*) practicing for many hours, George failed his driving test again.

   d. (*Although* / *Despite*) his mother and father spent hours with him in the car trying to teach him how to drive, George failed his driving test repeatedly.

   e. (*Although* / *Despite*) his mother and father's efforts to teach him how to drive, George failed his driving test.

4. a. (*Even though* / *In spite of*) repeated crop failures due to drought, the villagers are refusing to leave their traditional homeland for resettlement in other areas.

   b. (*Even though* / *In spite of*) their crops have failed repeatedly due to drought, the villagers are refusing to leave their traditional homeland for resettlement in other areas.

   c. The villagers refuse to leave (*even though* / *in spite of*) the drought.

   d. The villagers refuse to leave (*even though* / *in spite of*) the drought seriously threatens their food supply.

   e. The villagers refuse to leave (*even though* / *in spite of*) the threat to their food supply because of the continued drought.

   f. The villagers refuse to leave (*even though* / *in spite of*) the threat to their food supply is serious because of the continued drought.

   g. The villagers refuse to leave (*even though* / *in spite of*) their food supply is threatened.

   h. The villagers refuse to leave (*even though* / *in spite of*) their threatened food supply.

▶ **Practice 18. Showing contrast.** (Chart 19-6).
Complete the sentences with the letter of the correct phrase from the list.

    a. an inability to communicate well in any language besides English
    b. he had the necessary qualifications
    c. he is afraid of heights
    d. he is normally quite shy and sometimes inarticulate
    e. his fear of heights
    f. his parents were worried about his intelligence because he didn't speak until he was four years old
    g. it has been shown to be safe
    h. they have been shown to cause birth defects and sometimes death
    i. its many benefits
    j. his competence and experience

1. In spite of _____, Carl enjoyed his helicopter trip over the Grand Canyon in Arizona.

2. Although _____, Mark rode in a cable car to the top of Sugar Loaf mountain in Rio de Janeiro for the magnificent view.

3. Because of his age, John was not hired even though _____.

4. Although _____, many people avoid using a microwave oven for fear of its radiation.

5. Jack usually has little trouble making new friends in other countries despite _____.

6. In spite of _____, the use of chemotherapy to treat cancer has many severe side effects.

7. Though _____, Bob managed to give an excellent presentation at the board meeting.

8. Jerry continued to be denied a promotion despite _____.

9. Dangerous pesticides are still used in many countries even though _____.

10. Despite the fact that Einstein turned out to be a genius, _____.

▶ **Practice 19. Showing contrast.** (Chart 19-6).
Combine the two sentences in *italics*. Add any other necessary punctuation.

1. *It was night. We could see the road very clearly.*

    a. Even though _____.

    b. Although _____.

    c. _____, but _____.

2. *Helen has a fear of heights. She enjoys skydiving.*

    a. Despite the fact that _____, _____.

    b. Despite _____, _____.

    c. _____; nevertheless _____.

3. *Millie has the flu. She is working at her computer.*

    a. Though _____, _____.

    b. _____, but _____ anyway.

    c. _____, but _____ still _____

    _____.

▶ **Practice 20. Showing direct contrast.** (Chart 19-7)
Connect the given ideas using the words in parentheses. Add punctuation and capital letters as necessary.

1. (*while*) red is bright and lively gray is a dull color

   _____ *Red is bright and lively, while gray is a dull color.* _____ OR

   _____ *While red is bright and lively, gray is a dull color.* _____

2. (*on the other hand*) Jane is insecure and unsure of herself her sister is full of self-confidence

   _____

3. (*while*) a rock is heavy a feather is light

   _____

4. (*however*) some children are unruly others are quiet and obedient

   _____

5. (*on the other hand*) language and literature classes are easy and enjoyable for Alex math and science courses are difficult for him

   _____

6. (*however*) strikes can bring improvements in wages and working conditions strikes can also cause loss of jobs and bankruptcy

   _____

▶ **Practice 21. Expressing condition: using *otherwise*.** (Chart 19-8.)
Write sentences with the same meaning by using ***otherwise***. Use a modal or phrasal modal in your sentence.

1. If I don't call my mother, she'll start worrying about me.

   _____ *I am going to have to (should / had better / must) call my mother. Otherwise, she'll* _____

   _____ *start worrying about me.* _____

2. If the bus doesn't come soon, we'll be late to work.

   _____

3. Unless you've made a reservation, you won't get seated at the restaurant.

   _____

4. If Beth doesn't stop complaining, she will lose the few friends she has.

   _____

5. You can't get on the plane unless you have a government-issued ID.

   _____

6. Louis can replace his driver's license only if he applies for it in person.

   _____

7. Only if you are a registered voter can you vote in the general election.

   _____

8. If you don't clean up the kitchen tonight, you'll have to clean it up early tomorrow.

   _____

▶ **Practice 22. Expressing cause and effect.** (Chart 19-9)
Complete the sentences in Column A with a phrase from Column B.

Column A

1. We see lightning first and then hear the thunder because _____.
2. Plants need light to live. These plants didn't have light; therefore, _____.
3. Halley's Comet appears in the sky every 76 years, so _____.
4. Children in Scandinavia go to school in darkness in the winter since _____.
5. Objects fall to the ground because of _____.
6. Now that _____, newspapers are not as necessary as they used to be.
7. People get their news faster than they used to due to _____.
8. Because _____, people can heat the air in a balloon and make it fly.

Column B

a. faster means of communication
b. gravity
c. hot air rises to the top
d. it will next be seen in 2061
e. light travels faster than sound
f. people can get their news instantly by computer or on TV
g. there is almost no daylight then
h. they died

▶ **Practice 23. Expressing contrast.** (Chart 19-9)
Circle the word(s) to complete the sentences.

1. Colombia exports a lot of emeralds, while South Africa (*exports / doesn't export*) gold.
2. Even though Colombia exports some precious stones, it (*exports / doesn't export*) diamonds.
3. Although Japan (*uses / doesn't use*) a lot of oil, oil isn't found in Japan.
4. Despite the declining population of Japan, Tokyo's population (*is / isn't*) getting larger.
5. Most people believe that the pineapple is native to Hawaii, a state in the middle of the Pacific Ocean; however, pineapples (*originated / didn't originate*) in South America.
6. China (*is / isn't*) the largest producer of pineapples today. Nevertheless, Hawaii still produces a lot of pineapples.

▶ **Practice 24. Expressing condition.** (Chart 19-9)
Write the correct form of the verb **pass** in each sentence.

1. Keith will graduate if he _____*passes*_____ all of his courses.
2. Sam won't graduate if he _____*doesn't pass*_____ all of his courses.

3. Ed won't graduate unless he _____ all of his courses.

4. Sue will graduate only if she _____ all of her courses.

5. Jessica will graduate even if she _____ all of her courses.

6. Alex won't graduate even if he _____ all of his courses.

7. Jennifer will graduate unless she _____ all of her courses.

▶ **Practice 25. Summary of connectives: cause and effect, contrast, condition.**
(Chart 19-9)

Complete the sentences logically using the ideas in the list. Write each verb in its correct tense.

    a. take care of the garden (or not)
    b. the flowers bloom (or not)
    c. my care

Punctuate and capitalize correctly.

1. Because I took good care of the garden, _____*the flowers bloomed*_____.

2. The flowers bloomed because _____*I took good care of the garden*_____.

3. The flowers bloomed because of _____*my care*_____.

4. The flowers didn't bloom in spite of _____.

5. Although I took good care of the garden _____.

6. I did not take good care of the garden therefore _____.

7. I didn't take good care of the garden however _____.

8. I took good care of the garden nevertheless _____.

9. I did not take good care of the garden so _____.

10. Even though I did not take good care of the garden _____.

11. Since I did not take good care of the garden _____.

12. I didn't take good care of the garden, but _____ anyway.

13. If I take good care of the garden _____.

14. Unless I take good care of the garden _____.

15. I must take good care of the garden otherwise _____.

16. I did not take good care of the garden consequently _____.

17. I did not take good care of the garden nonetheless _____.

18. I have to take good care of the garden so that _____.

19. Only if I take good care of the garden _____.

20. I took good care of the garden yet _____.

21. You'd better take good care of the garden or else _____.

22. The flowers will probably bloom whether _____.

Chapter 20
Conditional Sentences and Wishes

▶ **Practice 1. Introduction to conditional sentences.** (Chart 20-1)
Read the sentences under the *italicized* sentence. Circle *yes* if the sentence describes the situation. Circle *no* if the sentence doesn't describe the situation.

1. *If Sally didn't have the flu, she would be at work today.*
   a. Sally has the flu.   yes   no
   b. Sally is at work today.   yes   no

2. *If Albert didn't take his allergy medication, he would sneeze and cough all day.*
   a. Albert takes his allergy medication.   yes   no
   b. Albert sneezes and coughs all day.   yes   no

3. *If our first flight had been on time, we would not have missed our connecting flight.*
   a. The first flight was on time.   yes   no
   b. We missed our connecting flight.   yes   no

4. *If we had a reliable car, we would drive from the East Coast to the West Coast.*
   a. We have a reliable car.   yes   no
   b. We are going to drive from the East Coast to the West Coast   yes   no
   c. We would like to drive from the East Coast to the West Coast.   yes   no

5. *Tim would have married Tina if she had accepted his proposal of marriage.*
   a. Tina accepted Tim's marriage proposal.   yes   no
   b. Tina and Tim got married.   yes   no
   c. Tim wanted to marry Tina.   yes   no
   d. Tina wanted to marry Tom.   yes   no

▶ **Practice 2. Overview of basic verb forms in conditional sentences.**
       (Chart 20-1)
Complete each sentence according to its description. Write the letter of the correct completion.

Group 1.
   1. Present true: If it snows, __c__.   a. I would walk to work
   2. Present untrue: If it snowed, __a__.   b. I would have walked to work
                                                     c. I will walk to work
   3. Past untrue: If it had snowed, __b__.

Group 2.

1. Present true: If you come early, _____.

2. Present untrue: If you came early, _____.

3. Past untrue: If you had come early, _____.

a. we wouldn't be late
b. we wouldn't have been late
c. we won't be late

Group 3.

1. Present untrue: If Professor Smith were absent, _____.

2. Present true: If Professor Smith is absent, _____.

3. Past untrue: If Professor Smith had been absent, _____.

a. class would have been canceled
b. class will be canceled
c. class would be canceled

Group 4.

1. Present true: If John quits his job, _____.

2. Past untrue: If John had quit his job, _____.

3. Present untrue: If John quit his job, _____.

a. his wife will be upset
b. his wife would be upset
c. his wife would have been upset

▶ **Practice 3. True in the present or future.** (Chart 20-2)
Read the given sentence and the two sentences that follow. Complete the sentences with the verbs in the list.

| be, be | forget, look | heat, boil |
| eat, get | have, call | pet, purr |

1. Water boils at 100 degrees C. (212 degrees F.)

   (General truth) If you _____ water to 100 degrees C., it

   _____.

   (Future) If you _____ the water in that pot to 100 degrees C., it

   _____.

2. Sometimes I forget my own schedule.

   (Habitual activity) If I _____ my schedule, I _____ at

   my appointment calendar.

   (Future) If I _____ my schedule tomorrow, I _____

   at my appointment calendar.

3. Sometimes the cat purrs.

   (Habitual situation) If you _____ the cat gently, she

   _____.

   (Future) If you _____ the cat gently right now, she

   _____.

4. I might have some news tomorrow.

   (Future) If I _____ any news tomorrow, I _____ you.

   (Habitual situation) If I _____ any news, I _____

   you.

5. You eat too much junk food.

(Future) If you _____ too much junk food , you

_____ fat.

(Predictable fact) If you _____ too much junk food, you

_____ fat.

6. It might be cloudy tonight.

(Predictable fact) If it _____ cloudy, the stars _____

visible.

(Future) If it _____ cloudy tonight, the stars _____

visible.

▶ **Practice 4. Untrue (contrary to fact) in the present or future.** (Chart 20-3)
What is the true situation? Circle the letter of the sentence that describes the true situation.

1. If I had a million dollars, I would travel around the world.
   a. I have a million dollars.　　　b. I don't have a million dollars.

2. If I didn't have a bad cold, I'd go swimming with you.
   a. I have a bad cold.　　　b. I don't have a bad cold.

3. If Jenny were here, she could help us.
   a. Jenny is here.　　　b. Jenny isn't here.

4. If Henry weren't in charge here, nothing would ever get done.
   a. Henry is in charge here.　　　b. Henry isn't in charge here.

5. If I spoke Chinese, I could converse with your grandmother.
   a. I speak Chinese.　　　b. I don't speak Chinese.

6. If I knew the answer, I would tell you.
   a. I know the answer.　　　b. I don't know the answer.

▶ **Practice 5. Untrue (contrary to fact) in the present or future.** (Chart 20-3)
Read the given sentence(s) and the sentence that follows. Complete the second sentence with the verbs in the list.

| be, be | have, go | have, travel |
| be, can have | have, like | like, cook |

1. There aren't any trees on our street, and consequently, there is no shade.

   If there _____ trees on our street, there _____ shade.

2. We don't have enough money to travel abroad.

   If we _____ enough money, we _____ abroad.

3. The students don't have a good history teacher. They don't like history because of her.

   If the students _____ a better history teacher, they

   _____ history.

4. Sam doesn't like fish, so his mother doesn't cook it for him.

If Sam _____ fish, his mother _____ fish for him.

5. The weather is bad. We can't have our usual weekend picnic today.

If the weather _____ bad, we _____ our usual

weekend picnic today.

6. I have so much work to do. I will not go out with you tonight.

If I _____ so much work, I _____ out with you

tonight.

▶ **Practice 6. True vs. untrue in the present or future.** (Charts 20-2 and 20-3)
Complete the sentences in Column A with a clause in Column B.

Column A

1. If the temperature goes below freezing, _____.
2. If the temperature were below freezing right now, _____.
3. If the baby is hungry, _____.
4. If the baby were hungry, _____.
5. If this fish were not fresh, _____.
6. If fish is not fresh, _____.
7. If a car runs out of gas, _____.
8. If this car had more power, _____.
9. If you threw a rock into the water, _____.
10. If you throw a life ring into the water, _____.

Column B

a. it stops
b. he cries
c. it smells bad
d. we would be very cold
e. it would go faster
f. it floats
g. it would sink
h. we will be very cold
i. it would smell bad
j. he would cry

▶ **Practice 7. Untrue (contrary to fact) in the past.** (Chart 20-4)
Circle the letter of the sentence that describes the true situation.

1. If you had been here last night, you would have had a wonderful time. But _____.
   a. you were here   b. you weren't here

2. If I hadn't been rude, Jenna wouldn't have gotten angry. But _____.
   a. I was rude   b. I wasn't rude

3. If Anna hadn't been late, we could have seen the beginning of the movie. But _____.
   a. Anna was late   b. Anna wasn't late

4. If Henry hadn't fallen asleep, he wouldn't have crashed into the tree. But _____.
   a. he fell asleep   b. he didn't fall asleep

5. If Max had studied, he might have passed the test. But _____.
   a. he studied   b. he didn't study

6. If I had known the password, I would have told you. But _____.
   a. I knew the password   b. I didn't know the password

► **Practice 8. Untrue (contrary to fact) in the past.** (Chart 20-4)
Using the information in the first sentence, complete the conditional sentences with the correct form of the *italicized verbs.*

1. Adam met his future wife, Alice, on a flight to Tokyo.

   take, meet

   If Adam (*not*) _____ that flight to Tokyo, he (*not*) _____
   Alice.

2. I forgot my credit card, so I couldn't pay for my groceries.

   forget, can pay

   If I (*not*) _____ my credit card, I _____ for my
   groceries.

3. I didn't know Jane was in the hospital, so I didn't visit her.

   know, visit

   If I _____ that Jane was in the hospital, I _____ her.

4. Alex didn't pay the electric bill. The electric company cut off his power.

   pay, cut off

   If Alex _____ the bill, the electric company (*not*) _____
   his electricity.

5. The weather was bad. The outdoor concert was canceled.

   be, be

   If the weather _____ good, the outdoor concert (*not*)
   _____ canceled.

6. Alexander Fleming accidentally discovered the medical usefulness of a certain kind of mold.
   Scientists developed penicillin from that mold.

   discover, develop

   If Fleming (*not*) _____ that mold, scientists (*not*)
   _____ penicillin.

► **Practice 9. Conditional sentences: present, future, or past.** (Charts 20-2 → 20-4)
Write the letter of the correct phrase to complete each conversation.

a. I can join you	d. I had joined one
b. I could have joined you	e. I join one
c. I could join you	f. I joined one

1. A: Hi, Kim! Will you have lunch with us?

   B: I'm sorry, I can't. If ____, I would, but I have another appointment.

2. A: Hi, Sid! Say, will you have lunch with us tomorrow?

   B: Maybe. I might have to work through lunch, but if ____, I will.

3. A: Hey, Mary! What happened? Why didn't you have lunch with us?

   B: Oh, if ____, I would have, but I had an emergency at my office.

4. A: Mr. Simmons, you should exercise more.

   B: I'll try, Dr. Scott. Maybe I'll join a gym. If _____, I'll get more exercise.

5. A: Ms. Mora, you need to exercise. Why don't you join a gym?

   B: Oh, Doctor, if _____, it would be a waste of money. I would never use it.

6. A: Mrs. Smith, you said you were going to join a gym. You didn't!

   B: Right, I didn't. If _____, it would have been a waste of money. I would never have used it.

▶ **Practice 10. Conditional sentences: present, future, or past.** (Charts 20-2 → 20-4)
Write the correct form of the verbs in parentheses.

1. There's too much traffic these days. It's too bad we don't have wings. If we

   (*have*) _____ wings, we (*can, fly*) _____ over all this traffic

   instead of being stuck in it.

2. If we (*can, fly*) _____ over all this traffic, we (*arrive*) _____

   at our destination very quickly.

3. Maybe we'll get there before noon. If we (*get*) _____ there before noon, I

   (*have*) _____ a chance to talk with Olga before lunch.

4. I might have a chance to talk with Olga before we have lunch. If I (*have*) _____

   a chance to talk with Olga before we have lunch, I (*tell*) _____ her about

   the job opening in our department.

5. I didn't have a chance to talk to John yesterday. If I (*have*) _____ a chance to

   talk to him, I (*tell*) _____ him about the job opening.

6. You didn't tell John about the job opening at the meeting yesterday. But, even if you

   (*tell*) _____ him about the job opening, I'm sure that he

   (*be, not*) _____ interested at all. He's very happy with the job he has.

▶ **Practice 11. Conditional sentences.** (Charts 20-2 → 20-4)
Write a conditional sentence about each given sentence.

1. I was sick yesterday, so I didn't go to class.

   If _____*I hadn't been sick yesterday, I would have gone to class*_____.

2. Because Alan never eats breakfast, he always overeats at lunch.

   If _____.

3. Kostas was late to his own wedding because his watch was slow.

   If _____.

4. I don't ride the bus to work every morning because it's always so crowded.

   If _____.

5. Sara didn't know that Highway 57 was closed, so she didn't take an alternative route.

   If _____.

6. Camille couldn't finish unloading the truck because no one was there to help her.

   If _____.

▶ **Practice 12. Progressive verb forms in conditional sentences.**
(Chart 20-5)
Write a conditional sentence about each given sentence. Use *if*.

1. The wind is blowing so hard. We can't go sailing.

    If the wind weren't blowing so hard, we could go sailing.

2. The wind was blowing so hard. We couldn't go sailing.

    _____

3. The water is running. I can't hear you.

    _____

4. The water was running. I couldn't hear the phone.

    _____

5. The baby is hungry. That's why she's crying.

    _____

6. Dick was sleeping soundly so he didn't hear his alarm clock.

    _____

7. I was watching an exciting mystery on TV, so I didn't answer the phone.

    _____

8. I'm trying to concentrate, so I can't talk to you now.

    _____

▶ **Practice 13. Using "mixed time" in conditional sentences.** (Chart 20-6)
Circle the letters of the sentences that describe the situation.

1. If I hadn't stayed up late last night, I wouldn't be tired this morning.
    (a.) I went to bed late.
    b. I went to bed early.
    (c.) I am tired this morning.
    d. I am not tired this morning.

2. If Bob had saved some money, he could buy a house now.
    a. Bob saved some money.
    b. Bob didn't save any money.
    c. Bob can buy a house.
    d. Bob can't buy a house.

3. If I hadn't apologized to Ben, he would still be angry at me.
    a. I apologized to Ben.
    b. I didn't apologize to Ben.
    c. Ben is still angry at me.
    d. Ben is not angry at me anymore.

4. If I had taken Grandpa's advice, I wouldn't be in this mess now!
    a. I took Grandpa's advice.
    b. I didn't take Grandpa's advice.
    c. I am in a mess now.
    d. I am not in a mess now.

5. If Laura hadn't been wearing her seat belt, she would have been severely injured.
   a. Laura was wearing her seat belt.
   b. Laura wasn't wearing her seat belt.
   c. Laura was severely injured.
   d. Laura was not severely injured.

6. If new houses had not been built near the campgrounds, the area would still be wilderness.
   a. New houses have been built near the campgrounds.
   b. New houses have not been built near the campgrounds.
   c. The area is still wilderness.
   d. The area is not wilderness anymore.

▶ **Practice 14. Using progressive forms and "mixed time" in conditional sentences.** (Charts 20-5 and 20-6)

Write a conditional sentence about each given sentence.

1. It is raining, so we won't finish the game.

   If _____ *it weren't raining, we would finish the game* _____.

2. I didn't eat lunch, and now I'm hungry.

   If _____.

3. Bob left his wallet at home this morning, and now he doesn't have money for lunch.

   If _____.

4. Bruce is always daydreaming, and so he never gets his work done.

   If _____.

5. My muscles hurt today because I played basketball for three hours last night.

   If _____.

6. I couldn't hear what you said because the band was playing so loud.

   If _____.

7. Because Diane asked the technician a lot of questions, she understands how to use her computer now.

   If _____.

8. Olga and Ivan weren't paying attention, so they didn't see the exit sign on the highway.

   If _____.

9. I really don't know what the test results mean because the doctor didn't explain them to me.

   If _____.

10. We were sleeping last night, so we didn't hear the thunder and lightning.

    If _____.

▶ Practice 15. Omitting *if*. (Chart 20-7)

Write sentences with the same meaning by omitting *if*.

1. If I were you, I wouldn't go there.

   _____Were I_____ you, I wouldn't go there.

2. If you should need my help, please call.

   _____Should you need_____ my help, please call.

3. If I had known about her accident, I would have gone to the hospital immediately.

   _____ about her accident, I would have gone to the hospital

   immediately.

4. If I had been offered a job at the law office, I would have gladly accepted.

   _____ a job at the law office, I would have gladly accepted.

5. If anyone should call, would you please take a message?

   _____, would you please take a message?

6. Directions on the pizza box: "If this pizza needs reheating, place it in a hot oven for five minutes."

   _____, place it in a hot oven for five minutes.

7. Directions on a medicine bottle: "If you feel any dizziness, nausea, or muscle pain, discontinue taking this medicine and call your doctor immediately."

   _____ any dizziness, nausea, or muscle pain, discontinue taking this

   medicine and call your doctor immediately.

8. If you were really a lawyer, I would take your advice.

   _____, I would take your advice.

▶ Practice 16. Omitting *if*. (Chart 20-7)

Circle the letter of the one sentence that has the same meaning as the given sentence.

1. Had I seen the hole in the sidewalk, I wouldn't have tripped and fallen down.
   a. I had to see the hole in the sidewalk.
   b. I saw the hole in the sidewalk.
   c. I didn't see the hole in the sidewalk.
   d. I didn't fall down.

2. Should you have further questions, please don't hesitate to contact us again.
   a. You should ask more questions.
   b. You might have more questions.
   c. You will certainly have more questions.
   d. Don't bother calling us again.

3. Had the building been properly built, it would have withstood the hurricane.
   a. The building was properly built.
   b. The building survived the hurricane.
   c. The building wasn't properly built.
   d. The building was built after the hurricane.

4. Were you rich, you could fly across the ocean to visit your family every week.
   a. Are you rich?
   b. You are not rich.
   c. You visit your family every week.
   d. You used to be rich, but you are not anymore.

▶ **Practice 17. Implied conditions.** (Chart 20-8)
Complete the sentences with *if*-clauses.

1. Sara's dad would have picked her up, but I forgot to tell him that she needed a ride.

   Sara's dad would have picked her up if _I hadn't forgotten to tell him that she needed a ride_ .

2. I couldn't have finished the project without your help.

   I couldn't have finished the project if _____.

3. I opened the door slowly. Otherwise, I could have hit someone.

   If _____, I could have hit someone.

4. Doug would have gone on vacation with me, but he couldn't get time off from work.

   Doug would have gone with me if _____.

5. CAROL: Why didn't Oscar tell his boss about the problem?

   ALICE: He would have gotten into a lot of trouble.

   Oscar would have gotten into a lot of trouble if _____

   _____.

▶ **Practice 18. Review: conditional sentences.** (Charts 20-1 → 20-8)
Write the letter of the correct completion for each sentence.

1. If I could speak Spanish, I _____ next year studying in Spain.
   a. will spend   c. had spent
   b. would have spent   d. would spend

2. It would have been a much more serious accident _____ fast at the time.
   a. had she been driving   c. she had driven
   b. was she driving   d. if she drove

3. A: Can I borrow your car for this evening?
   B: Sure, but Nora's using it right now. If she _____ it back in time, you're welcome to borrow it.
   a. brought   c. brings
   b. would bring   d. will bring

4. I didn't get home until well after midnight last night. Otherwise, I _____ your call.
   a. returned   c. would return
   b. had returned   d. would have returned

5. If energy _____ inexpensive and unlimited, many things in the world would be different.
   a. is   c. were
   b. will be   d. would be

6. We _____ the game if we'd had a few more minutes.
    a. will win
    b. won
    c. had won
    d. could have won

7. I _____ William with me if I had known you and he didn't get along with each other.
    a. hadn't brought
    b. didn't bring
    c. wouldn't have brought
    d. won't bring

8. Dr. Mason was out of town, so a guest lecturer gave the talk. It was boring and I almost fell asleep. If Dr. Mason _____, I would have paid attention and not fallen asleep.
    a. lectured
    b. had been lecturing
    c. was lecturing
    d. would lecture

9. If you _____ to my advice in the first place, you wouldn't be in this mess right now.
    a. listen
    b. had listened
    c. will listen
    d. listened

10. _____ interested in that subject, I would try to learn more about it.
    a. Were I
    b. Should I
    c. I was
    d. If I am

11. If I _____ the problems you had as a child, I might not have succeeded in life as well as you have.
    a. have
    b. would have
    c. had had
    d. should have

12. I _____ your mother to dinner if I had known she was visiting you.
    a. invite
    b. invited
    c. had invited
    d. would have invited

13. _____ more help, I can call my neighbor.
    a. Needed
    b. Should I need
    c. I have needed
    d. I should need

14. _____ then what I know today, I would have saved myself a lot of time and trouble over the years.
    a. If I know
    b. Did I know
    c. If I would know
    d. Had I known

15. Do you think there would be less conflict in the world if all people _____ the same language?
    a. speak
    b. will speak
    c. spoke
    d. had spoken

16. If you can tell me why I wasn't included, _____ this incident again.
    a. I don't mention
    b. I will never mention
    c. I never mention
    d. will I never mention

17. I didn't know you were asleep. Otherwise, I _____ so much noise when I came in.
    a. didn't make
    b. wouldn't have made
    c. won't make
    d. don't make

18. Unless you _____ all of my questions, I can't do anything to help you.
    a. answered
    b. answer
    c. would answer
    d. are answering

19. Had you told me that this was going to happen, I _____ it.
   a. never would have believed   c. hadn't believed
   b. don't believe   d. can't believe

20. If Jake _____ to go on the trip, would you have gone alone?
   a. doesn't agree   c. hadn't agreed
   b. didn't agree   d. wouldn't agree

▶ **Practice 19. Verb forms following *wish*.** (Chart 20-9)
Circle the letter of the sentence that describes the true situation.

1. I wish that you were my true friend.
   a. You are my true friend.
   b. You are not my true friend.

2. I wish I had known the truth.
   a. I knew the truth.
   b. I didn't know the truth.

3. I wish you hadn't lied to me.
   a. You lied to me.
   b. You didn't lie to me.

4. I wish we were going on vacation.
   a. We are going on vacation.
   b. We are not going on vacation.

5. I wish I had a motorcycle.
   a. I have a motorcycle.
   b. I don't have a motorcycle.

6. I wish John could have met my father.
   a. John was able to meet my father.
   b. John was not able to meet my father.

▶ **Practice 20. Verb forms following *wish*.** (Chart 20-9)
Make wishes. Complete the sentences with a verb.

1. The sun isn't shining.

   I wish the sun _____*were shining*_____ right now.

2. You didn't go to the concert with us last night.

   I wish you _____ with us to the concert last night.

3. Spiro didn't drive to this party.

   I wish Spiro _____ to the party. I'd ask him for a ride home.

4. I can't swim.

   I wish I _____ so I would feel safe in a boat.

5. Our team didn't win.

   I wish our team _____ the game last night.

6. Bill didn't get the promotion.

   I wish Bill _____ the promotion. He feels bad.

7. I quit my job.

   I wish I _____ my job until I'd found another one.

8. It isn't winter.

   I wish it _____ winter so that I could go skiing.

9. Al probably won't sing for us because he's so shy. I wish Al _____ a

   couple of songs. He has a good voice.

▶ **Practice 21. Verb forms following _wish_.** (Chart 20-9)
Write the correct form of the verbs in parentheses.

1. Heinrich doesn't like his job as a house painter. He wishes he (_go_) _____ to art
   school when he was younger. He wishes he (_can, paint_) _____ canvasses
   instead of houses for a living.

2. I don't like living here. I wish I (_move, not_) _____ to this big city. I
   can't seem to make any friends, and everything is so crowded. I wish I (_take_) _____
   _____ the job I was offered before I moved here.

3. I know I shouldn't eat junk food every day, but I wish you (_stop_) _____
   nagging me about it.

4. I wish you (_invite, not_) _____ the neighbors over for dinner
   when you talked to them earlier this afternoon. I don't feel like cooking a big dinner.

5. A: Did you get your car back from the garage?
   B: Yes, and it still isn't fixed. I wish I (_pay, not_) _____ them in full
      when I picked up the car. I should have waited to be sure that everything was all right.

6. A: I wish you (_hurry_) _____! We're going to be late.
   B: I wish you (_relax_) _____. We've got plenty of time.

7. A: How do you like the new president of our neighborhood association?
   B: Not much. I wish she (_elect, not_) _____. I never should
      have voted for her.
   A: Oh, really? Then you probably wish I (_vote, not_) _____ for
      her either. If you recall, she won by only one vote. You and I could have changed the
      outcome of the election if we'd known then what we know now.

8. A: My thirteen-year-old daughter wishes she (_be, not_) _____ so tall and
      that her hair (_be_) _____ black and straight.
   B: Really? My daughter wishes she (_be_) _____ taller and that her hair
      (_be_) _____ blond and curly.

9. A: I can't go to the game with you this afternoon.
   B: Really? That's too bad. But I wish you (_tell_) _____ me sooner so that
      I could have invited someone else to go with me.

10. A: How long have you been sick?
    B: For over a week.
    A: I wish you (_go_) _____ to see a doctor later today. You should find out
       what's wrong with you.
    B: Maybe I'll go tomorrow.

▶ **Practice 22. Using *would* to make wishes about the future.** (Chart 20-10)
Complete the sentences. Make wishes about the future by writing ***would*** and a verb from the list.

| cook | end | get | hang up | leave | snow |

1. A: So, Mom, how do you like my haircut?

   B: You had a haircut? Your hair is still long. I wish you _____ a real
   haircut.

2. A: Aren't you going on your annual ski trip this year?

   B: No, not unless it snows. There hasn't been any snow this year. I wish it
   _____ so we could go skiing.

3. A: Helen! How long are our guests going to stay? It's almost midnight.

   B: I don't know. I wish they _____, but Henry just keeps on talking.
   Everyone is falling asleep.

4. A: I love you, Pat, but I wish you were neater.

   B: Neater? What do you mean? I pick up everything, I clean up everything . . .

   A: Well, I mean I wish you _____ your clothes instead of leaving them on
   a chair.

5. A: What's the matter? Don't you like the movie?

   B: Not at all! I wish it _____. We have to stay, though because the kids
   are enjoying it so much.

6. A: Meatballs again?

   B: Don't you like meatballs?

   A: You know I do, but sometimes I wish you _____ something else.

▶ **Practice 23. Conditionals.** (Chapter 20)
Complete the sentences. Write the correct form of the verb in parentheses.

TOM: What's wrong, Bob? You look awful!

BOB: Well, you (*look*) _____ bad too if you (*have*) _____ a day
   $\overline{1}$ $\overline{2}$
   like mine yesterday. My car slid into a tree because the roads were icy.

TOM: Oh? What happened?

BOB: Well, I suppose if I (*drive, not*) _____ so fast, I
   $\overline{3}$
   (*slide, not*) _____ into the tree.
   $\overline{4}$

TOM: Gosh, Bob, speeding again? Don't you know that if a driver (*step*)

   _____ on the gas on ice, the car will spin around in a circle?
   $\overline{5}$

Bob: I know that now, but I didn't know that yesterday! If I (know) _____
6

that yesterday, I (not, crash) _____ . And besides, I didn't
7

have my driver's license with me, so I'll have to pay an extra fine for that when I go to

court next month.

Tom: You were driving without your license?

Bob: Yeah. It slipped out of my pocket.

Tom: You sure have bad luck! Maybe if you (take, not) _____ that bus, you
8

(lose, not) _____ your wallet. If you (lose, not)
9

_____ your wallet, you (have) _____ your
10   11

driver's license with you when you hit a tree. If you (have) _____ your
12

license with you, you (have to pay, not) _____ a steep fine
13

when you go to court next week. And of course, if you (drive, not) _____
14

_____ too fast, you (run into, not) _____ a
15

tree, and you (be, not) _____ in this mess now. If I
16

(be) _____ you, I (take) _____ it easy and just
17   18

(stay) _____ home where you'll be no danger to yourself or to anyone else.
19

Bob: Enough about me! How about you?

Tom: Well, things are really looking up for me. I'm planning to take off for Florida soon.

I'm sick of all this cold, rainy weather. I (stay) _____ here for vacation
20

if the weather (be, not) _____ so bad. But I need some sun!
21

Bob: I wish I (can, go) _____ with you. How are you planning on getting
22

there?

Tom: If I have enough money, I (fly) _____ . Otherwise, I
23

(take) _____ the bus. I wish I (can, drive) _____
24   25

my own car there because it (be) _____ nice to have it to drive around
26

in once I get there, but it's such a long trip. I wish I (have) _____ someone
27

to go with me and share the driving.

Bob: Hey, what about me? Why don't I go with you? I can share the driving. I'm a great

driver!

Tom: Didn't you just get through telling me that you'd wrapped your car around a tree?

Appendix
Supplementary Grammar Units

▶ **Practice 1. Subjects, verbs, and objects.** (Chart A-1)
Underline and identify the subject (**s**), verb (**v**), and object of the verb (**o**) in each sentence.

           s   **v**   **o**
1. Airplanes have wings.

2. The teacher explained the problem.

3. Children enjoy games.

4. Jack wore a blue suit.

5. Some animals eat plants. Some animals eat other animals.

6. According to an experienced waitress, you can carry full cups of coffee without spilling them

    just by never looking at them.

▶ **Practice 2. Transitive vs. intransitive verbs.** (Chart A-1)
Underline and identify the verb in each sentence. Write **VT** if it is transitive. Write **VI** if it is intransitive.

           VI
1. Alice arrived at six o'clock.
           VT
2. We drank some tea.

3. I agree with you.

4. I waited for Sam at the airport for two hours.

5. They're staying at a resort hotel in San Antonio, Texas.

6. Mr. Chan is studying English.

7. The wind is blowing hard today.

8. I walked to the theater, but Janice rode her bicycle.

9. Crocodiles hatch from eggs.

10. Rivers flow toward the sea.

▶ **Practice 3. Adjectives and adverbs.** (Charts A-2 and A-3)
Underline and identify the adjectives (**ADJ**) and adverbs (**ADV**) in these sentences.

                    ADJ   **ADV**
1. Jack opened the heavy door slowly.

2. Chinese jewelers carved beautiful ornaments from jade.

3. The old man carves wooden figures skillfully.

4. A busy executive usually has short conversations on the telephone.

5. The young woman had a very good time at the picnic yesterday.

▶ **Practice 4. Adjectives and adverbs.** (Charts A-2 and A-3)
Complete each sentence with the correct adjective or adverb.

1. *quick, quickly*   We ate ____*quickly*____ and ran to the theater.

2. *quick, quickly*   We had a ____*quick*____ dinner and ran to the theater.

3. *polite, politely*   I've always found Fred to be a _____ person.

4. *polite, politely*   He responded to my question _____ .

5. *regular, regularly*   Mr. Thomas comes to the store _____ for cheese and bread.

6. *regular, regularly*   He is a _____ customer.

7. *usual, usually*   The teacher arrived at the _____ time.

8. *usual, usually*   She _____ comes to class five minutes before it begins.

9. *good, well*   Jennifer Cooper paints _____ .

10. *good, well*   She is a _____ artist.

11. *gentle, gently*   A _____ breeze touched my face.

12. *gentle, gently*   A breeze _____ touched my face.

13. *bad, badly*   The audience booed the actors' _____ performance.

14. *bad, badly*   The audience booed and whistled because the actors performed _____ throughout the show.

▶ **Practice 5. Midsentence adverbs.** (Chart A-3)
Put the adverb in parentheses in its usual midsentence position.

                         always

1. (*always*)   Sue ∧ takes a walk in the morning.

2. (*always*)   Tim is a hard worker.

3. (*always*)   Beth has worked hard.

4. (*always*)   Jack works hard.

5. (*always*)   Do you work hard?

6. (*usually*)   Taxis are available at the airport.

7. (*rarely*)   Yusef takes a taxi to his office.

8. (*often*)   I have thought about quitting my job and sailing to Alaska.

9. (*probably*)   Yuko needs some help.

10. (*ever*)   Have you attended the show at the Museum of Space?

11. (*seldom*)   Al goes out to eat at a restaurant.

12. (*hardly ever*)   The students are late.

13. (*usually*)   Do you finish your homework before dinner?

14. (*generally*)   In India, the monsoon season begins in April.

15. (*usually*)   During the monsoon season, Mr. Singh's hometown receives around

                         610 centimeters (240 inches) of rain, which is an unusually large amount.

▶ **Practice 6. Identifying prepositions.** (Chart A-4)
<u>Underline</u> the prepositions.

1. Jim came to class <u>without</u> his books.
2. We stayed at home during the storm.
3. Sonya walked across the bridge over the Cedar River.
4. When Alex walked through the door, his little sister ran toward him and put her arms around his neck.
5. The two of us need to talk to Tom too.
6. Animals live in all parts of the world. Animals walk or crawl on land, fly in the air, and swim in the water.
7. Scientists divide living things into two main groups: the animal kingdom and the plant kingdom.
8. Asia extends from the Pacific Ocean in the east to Africa and Europe in the west.

▶ **Practice 7. Sentence elements.** (Charts A-1 → A-4)
Underline and identify the subject (**S**), verb (**V**), object (**O**), and prepositional phrases (**PP**) in the following sentences.

     S   V   O   PP
1. Jack put the letter in the mailbox.

2. The children walked to school.

3. Mary did her homework at the library.

4. Chinese printers created the first paper money in the world.

5. Dark clouds appeared on the horizon.

6. Mary filled the shelves of the cabinet with boxes of old books.

▶ **Practice 8. Linking verbs.** (Chart A-6)
Some of the *italicized* words in the following are used as linking verbs. Identify which ones are linking verbs by underlining them. Also underline the adjective that follows the linking verb.

1. Olga *looked* at the fruit. *(no underline)*

2. It *looked* fresh.

3. Dan *noticed* a scratch on the door of his car.

4. Morris *tasted* the candy.

5. It *tasted* good.

6. The crowd *grew* quiet as the official began her speech.

7. Felix *grows* tomatoes in his garden.

8. Sally *grew* up in Florida.

9. I can *smell* the chicken in the oven.

10. It *smells* delicious.

11. Barbara *got* a package in the mail.

12. Al *got* sleepy after dinner.

13. During the storm, the sea *became* rough.

14. Nicole *became* a doctor after many years of study.

15. Diana *sounded* her horn to warn the driver of the other car.

16. Helen *sounded* happy when I talked to her.

17. The weather *turns* hot in July.

18. When Bob entered the room, I *turned* around to look at him.

19. I *turned* a page in the book.

20. It *appears* certain that Mary Hanson will win the election.

21. Dick's story *seems* strange. Do you believe it?

▶ **Practice 9. Linking verbs; adjectives and adverbs.** (Charts A-2 → A-6)
Complete each sentence with the correct adjective or adverb.

1. *clean, cleanly*   The floor looks ____*clean*____ .

2. *slow, slowly*   The bear climbed ____*slowly*____ up the tree.

3. *safe, safely*   The plane landed _____ on the runway.

4. *anxious, anxiously*   When the wind started to blow, I grew _____ .

5. *complete, completely*   This list of names appears _____ . No more names need to be added.

6. *wild, wildly*   The crowd yelled _____ when we scored a goal.

7. *honest, honestly*   The clerk looked _____ , but she wasn't. I discovered when I got home that she had cheated me.

8. *thoughtful, thoughtfully* Jane looked at her book _____ before she answered the teacher's question.

9. *good, well*   Most of the students did _____ on their tests.

10. *fair, fairly*   The contract offer sounded _____ to me, so I accepted the job.

11. *terrible, terribly*   Jim felt _____ about forgetting his son's birthday.

12. *good, well*   A rose smells _____ .

13. *light, lightly*   As dawn approached, the sky became _____ .

14. *confident, confidently*   Beth spoke _____ when she delivered her speech.

15. *famous, famously*   The actor became _____ throughout much of the world.

16. *fine, finely*   I don't think this milk is spoiled. It tastes _____ to me.

► **Practice 10. Review: basic question forms.** (Chart B-1)

From the underlined sentences, make questions for the given answers. Fill in the blank spaces with the appropriate words. If no word is needed, write Ø.

1. *Bob can live there.*

	Question word	Auxiliary verb	Subject	Main verb	Rest of question	→	Answer
1a.	Ø	Can	Bob	live	there	? →	Yes.
1b.	Where	can	Bob	live	Ø	? →	There.
1c.	Who	can	Ø	live	there	? →	Bob.

2. *Ron is living there.*

	Question word	Auxiliary verb	Subject	Main verb	Rest of question	→	Answer
2a.	Ø				there	? →	Yes.
2b.	Where				Ø	? →	There.
2c.	Who				there	? →	Ron.

3. *Sue lives there.*

	Question word	Auxiliary verb	Subject	Main verb	Rest of question	→	Answer
3a.	Ø				there	? →	Yes.
3b.	Where				Ø	? →	There.
3c.	Who				there	? →	Sue.

4. *Ann will live there.*

	Question word	Auxiliary verb	Subject	Main verb	Rest of question	→	Answer
4a.	Ø				there	? →	Yes.
4b.	Where				Ø	? →	There.
4c.	Who				there	? →	Ann.

5. *Jack lived there.*

	Question word	Auxiliary verb	Subject	Main verb	Rest of question	→	Answer
5a.					there	? →	Yes.
5b.					Ø	? →	There.
5c.					there	? →	Jack.

6. *Mary has lived there.*

	Question word	Auxiliary verb	Subject	Main verb	Rest of question	→	Answer
6a.						? →	Yes.
6b.						? →	There.
6c.						? →	Mary.

▶ **Practice 11. Yes / no and information questions.** (Charts B-1 and B-2)
Make questions to fit the conversations. Notice in the examples that there is a short answer and then in parentheses a long answer. Your questions should produce those answers.

1. A: _____*When are you going to the zoo?*_____

    B: Tomorrow. (*I'm going to the zoo tomorrow.*)

2. A: _____*Are you going downtown later today?*_____

    B: Yes. (*I'm going downtown later today.*)

3. A: _____

    B: Yes. (*I live in an apartment.*)

4. A: _____

    B: In a condominium. (*Sue lives in a condominium.*)

5. A: _____

    B: Jack. (*Jack lives in that house.*)

6. A: _____

    B: Yes. (*I can speak French.*)

7. A: _____

    B: Ron. (*Ron can speak Arabic.*)

8. A: _____

    B: Two weeks ago. (*Olga arrived two weeks ago.*)

9. A: _____

    B: Ali. (*Ali arrived late.*)

10. A: _____

    B: The window. (*Ann is opening the window.*)

11. A: _____

    B: Opening the window. (*Ann is opening the window.*)

12. A: _____

    B: Her book. (*Mary opened her book.*)

13. A: _____

    B: Tom. (*Tom opened the door.*)

14. A: _____

    B: Yes. (*The mail has arrived.*)

15. A: _____

    B: Yes. (*I have a bicycle.*)

16. A: _____

    B: A pen. (*Alex has a pen in his hand.*)

17. A: _____

    B: Yes. (*I like ice cream.*)

18. A: _____

    B: Yes. (*I would like an ice cream cone.*)

19. A: _____

    B: A candy bar. (*Joe would like a candy bar.*)

20. A: _____

    B: Ann. (*Ann would like a soft drink.*)

▶ **Practice 12. Information questions.** (Charts B-1 and B-2)
Make questions from these sentences. The *italicized* words in parentheses should be the answers to your questions.

1. I take my coffee (*black*). → *How do you take your coffee?*

2. I have (*an English-Spanish*) dictionary.

3. He (*runs a grocery store*) for a living.

4. Margaret was talking to (*her uncle*).

5. (*Only ten*) people showed up for the meeting.

6. (*Because of heavy fog*), none of the planes could take off.

7. She was thinking about (*her experiences as a rural doctor*).

8. I was driving (*sixty-five miles per hour*) when the police officer stopped me.

9. I like (*hot and spicy Mexican*) food best.

10. (*The*) apartment (*at the end of the hall on the second floor*) is mine.

11. Oscar is (*friendly, generous, and kindhearted*).

12. Oscar is (*tall and thin and has short black hair*).

13. (*Ann's*) dictionary fell to the floor.

14. Abby isn't here (*because she has a doctor's appointment*).

15. All of the students in the class will be informed of their final grades (*on Friday*).

16. I feel (*awful*).

17. Of those three books, I preferred (*the one by Tolstoy*).

18. I like (*rock*) music.

19. The plane is expected to be (*an hour*) late.

20. The driver of the stalled car lit a flare (*in order to warn oncoming cars*).

21. I want (*the felt-tip*) pen, (*not the ballpoint*).

22. The weather is (*hot and humid*) in July.

23. I like my steak (*medium rare*).

24. I did (*very well*) on the test.

25. There are (*31,536,000*) seconds in a year.

▶ **Practice 13. Information questions.** (Charts B-1 and B-2)
Make questions from the following sentences. The words in parentheses should be the answers to your questions.

1. I need (*five dollars*). → *How much money do you need?*

2. Roberto was born (*in Panama*).

3. I go out to eat (*at least once a week*).

4. I'm waiting for (*Maria*).

5. (*My sister*) answered the phone.

6. I called (*Benjamin*).

7. (*Benjamin*) called.

8. She bought (*twelve gallons of*) gas.

9. *Deceitful* means ("*dishonest*").

10. An abyss is (*a bottomless hole*).

11. He went (*this*) way, (*not that way*).

12. These are (*Jim's*) books and papers.

13. They have (*four*) children.

14. He has been here (*for two hours*).

15. It is (*two hundred miles*) to Madrid.

16. The doctor can see you (*at three on Friday*).

17. Her roommate is (*Jane Peters*).

18. Her roommates are (*Jane Peters and Sue Lee*).

19. My parents have been living there (*for three years*).

20. This is (*Alice's*) book.

21. (*Fred and Jack*) are coming over for dinner.

22. Ann's dress is (*blue*).

23. Ann's eyes are (*brown*).

24. (*Bob*) can't go on the picnic.

25. Bob can't go (*because he is sick*).

26. I didn't answer the phone (*because I didn't hear it ring*).

27. I like (*classical*) music.

28. I don't understand (*the chart on page 50*).

29. Janet is (*studying*) right now.

30. You spell *sitting* (*with two "t's"—S-I-T-T-I-N-G*).

31. Tom (*is about medium height and has red hair and freckles*).

32. Tom is (*very serious and hard-working*).

33. Ron (*works as a civil engineer for the railroad company*).

34. Mexico is (*eight hundred miles*) from here.

35. I take my coffee (*black with sugar*).

36. Of Stockholm and Moscow, (*Stockholm*) is farther north.

37. (*Fine.*) I'm getting along (*just fine*).

▶ Practice 14. Negative questions. (Chart B-4)

In these dialogues, make negative questions from the words in parentheses, and determine the expected response.

1. A: Your infected finger looks terrible. (*you, see, not*) __Haven't you seen__ a doctor yet?

   B: __No__. But I'm going to. I don't want the infection to get any worse.

2. A: You look pale. What's the matter? (*you, feel*) _____ well?

   B: _____. I think I might be coming down with something.

3. A: Did you see Mark at the meeting?

   B: No, I didn't.

   A: Really? (*he, be, not*) _____ there?

   B: _____.

   A: That's funny. I've never known him to miss a meeting before.

4. A: Why didn't you come to the meeting yesterday afternoon?

   B: What meeting? I didn't know there was a meeting.

   A: (*Mary, tell, not*) _____ you about it?

   B: _____. No one said a word to me about it.

5. A: I have a package for Janet. (*Janet and you, work, not*) _____ _____ in the same building?

   B: _____. I'd be happy to take the package to her tomorrow when I go to work.

6. A: Frank didn't report all of his income on his tax forms.

   B: (*that, be, not*) _____ against the law?

   A: _____. And that's why he's in a lot of legal trouble. He might even go to jail.

7. A: Did you give Linda my message when you went to class this morning?

   B: No. I didn't see her.

   A: Oh? (*she, be*) _____ in class?

   B: _____. She didn't come today.

8. A: Do you see that woman over there, the one in the blue dress? (*she, be*) _____ Mrs. Robbins?

   B: _____ .

   A: I thought so. I wonder what she is doing here.

▶ **Practice 15. Tag questions.** (Chart B-5)
Add tag questions to the following.

1. You live in an apartment, ___*don't you*___ ?

2. You've never been in Italy, ___*have you*___ ?

3. Sally turned in her report, _____ ?

4. There are more countries north of the equator than south of it, _____ ?

5. You've never met Jack Freeman, _____ ?

6. You have a ticket to the game, _____ ?

7. You'll be there, _____ ?

8. Tom knows Alice Reed, _____ ?

9. We should call Rita, _____ ?

10. Ostriches can't swim, _____ ?

11. These books aren't yours, _____ ?

12. That's Bob's, _____ ?

13. Your neighbors died in the accident, _____ ?

14. I'm right, _____ ?

15. This grammar is easy, _____ ?

▶ **Practice 16. Contractions.** (Chart C)
Write the contraction of the pronoun and verb if appropriate. Write Ø if the pronoun and verb cannot be contracted.

1. He is (___*He's*___) in my class.

2. He was (___Ø___) in my class.

3. He has (___*He's*___) been here since July.

4. He has (___Ø___) a Volvo.★

★NOTE: **has, have,** and **had** are NOT contracted when they are used as main verbs. They are contracted only when they are used as helping verbs.

5. She had (_____) been there for a long time before we arrived.

6. She had (_____) a bad cold.

7. She would (_____) like to go to the zoo.

8. I did (_____) well on the test.

9. We will (_____) be there early.

10. They are (_____) in their seats over there.*

11. It is (_____) going to be hot tomorrow.

12. It has (_____) been a long time since I've seen him.

13. A bear is a large animal. It has (_____) four legs and brown hair.

14. We were (_____) on time.

15. We are (_____) always on time.

16. She has (_____) a good job.

17. She has (_____) been working there for a long time.

18. She had (_____) opened the window before class began.

19. She would (_____) have helped us if we had (_____) asked her.

20. He could (_____) have helped us if he had (_____) been there.

▶ **Practice 17. Using *not* and *no*.** (Chart D-1)
Change each sentence into the negative in two ways: use ***not . . . any*** in one sentence and ***no*** in the other.

1. I have some problems. → *I don't have any problems. I have no problems.*

2. There was some food on the shelf.

3. I received some letters from home.

4. I need some help.

5. We have some time to waste.

6. You should have given the beggar some money.

7. I trust someone. → *I don't trust anyone. I trust no one.***

8. I saw someone.

9. There was someone in his room.

10. She can find somebody who knows about it.

*****They're, their,** and **there** all have the same pronunciation.
******Also spelled with a hyphen in British English: *no-one*

▶ **Practice 18. Avoiding double negatives.** (Chart D-2)
Correct the errors in these sentences, all of which contain double negatives.

1. We don't have no time to waste.

   → *We have no time to waste.* OR *We don't have any time to waste.*

2. I didn't have no problems.

3. I can't do nothing about it.

4. You can't hardly ever understand her when she speaks.

5. I don't know neither Ann nor her husband.

6. Don't never drink water from that river without boiling it first.

7. Because I had to sit in the back row of the auditorium, I couldn't barely hear the speaker.

▶ **Practice 19. Beginning a sentence with a negative word.** (Chart D-3)
Change each sentence so that it begins with a negative word.

1. I had hardly stepped out of bed when the phone rang.

   → *Hardly had I stepped out of bed when the phone rang.*

2. I will never say that again.

3. I have scarcely ever enjoyed myself more than I did yesterday.

4. She rarely makes a mistake.

5. I will never trust him again because he lied to me.

6. It is hardly ever possible to get an appointment to see him.

7. I seldom skip breakfast.

8. I have never known a more generous person than Samantha.

▶ **Practice 20. Preposition combinations.** (Chart E)
Choose <u>all</u> the correct completions for each sentence.

1. Max is known for his (*honesty*) / *fairness*) / *famous*).

2. Several students were absent from (*yesterday* / *school* / *class*).

3. Has Maya recovered from (*her illness* / *her husband's death* / *the chair*)?

4. The criminal escaped from (*jail* / *the key* / *prison*).

5. Do you believe in (*ghosts* / *UFOs* / *scary*)?

6. Anthony is engaged to (*my cousin* / *a friend* / *marriage*).

7. Chris excels in (*mathematics* / *sports* / *his cousins*).

8. I'm very fond of (*you* / *exciting* / *your children*).

9. Henry doesn't approve of (*smoking* / *cigarettes* / *rain*).

10. I subscribe to (*magazines* / *a newspaper* / *websites*).

▶ **Practice 21. Preposition combinations.** (Chart E)
Choose the correct prepositions in parentheses.

1. Water consists (*of* / *with*) oxygen and hydrogen.

2. I am uncomfortable because that man is staring (*to* / *at*) me.

3. Ella hid the candy (*from* / *back*) the children.

4. I arrived (*in* / *to*) this country two weeks ago.

5. We arrived (*to* / *at*) the airport ten minutes late.

6. I am envious (*in* / *of*) people who can speak three or four languages fluently.

7. The students responded (*at* / *to*) the teacher's questions.

8. The farmers are hoping (*on* / *for*) rain.

9. I'm depending (*on* / *in*) you to finish this work for me.

10. Tim wore sunglasses to protect his eyes (*for* / *from*) the sun.

▶ **Practice 22. Preposition combinations.** (Chart E)
Complete the sentences with appropriate prepositions.

SITUATION 1: Mr. and Mrs. Jones just celebrated their 50th wedding anniversary.

1. They have been married ____*to*____ each other for 50 years.

2. They have always been faithful _____ each other.

3. They are proud _____ their marriage.

4. They are polite _____ one another.

5. They are patient _____ each other.

6. They are devoted _____ one another.

7. They have been committed _____ their marriage.

SITUATION 2: Jacob and Emily have been together for five months. They don't have a healthy relationship, and it probably won't last long.

1. They are often annoyed _____ each other's behavior.

2. They argue _____ each other every day.

3. They are bored _____ their relationship.

4. They are tired _____ one another.

5. Jacob is jealous _____ Emily's friends.

6. Emily is sometimes frightened _____ Jacob's moods.

▶ **Practice 23. Preposition combinations.** (Chart E)
Complete each sentence in Column A with the correct phrase from Column B.

Column A

1. My boots are made __c__ .

2. We hope you succeed ____ .

3. She forgave him ____ .

4. I'm going to take care ____ .

5. The firefighters rescued many people ____ .

6. I pray ____ .

7. Trucks are prohibited ____ .

Column B

a. from the burning building

b. for telling a lie

✓c. of leather

d. from entering the tunnel

e. in winning the scholarship

f. of the children tonight

g. for peace

▶ **Practice 24. Preposition combinations.** (Chart E)
Complete the sentences with appropriate prepositions.

1. Andrea contributed her ideas ____to____ the discussion.

2. Ms. Ballas substituted _____ our regular teacher.

3. I can't distinguish one twin _____ the other.

4. Children rely _____ their parents for food and shelter.

5. I'm worried _____ this problem.

6. I don't care _____ spaghetti. I'd rather eat something else.

7. Charles doesn't seem to care _____ his bad grades.

8. I'm afraid I don't agree _____ you.

9. We decided _____ eight o'clock as the time we should meet.

10. I am not familiar _____ that author's works.

11. Do you promise to come? I'm counting _____
    you to be here.

12. The little girl is afraid _____ an imaginary bear

    that lives in her closet.

▶ Practice 25. Preposition combinations. (Chart E)

Complete the sentences with appropriate prepositions.

1. We will fight _____*for*_____ our rights.

2. Who did you vote _____ in the last election?

3. Jason was late because he wasn't aware _____ the time.

4. I am grateful _____ you _____ your assistance.

5. Elena is not content _____ the progress she is making.

6. Paul's comments were not relevant _____ the topic under discussion.

7. Have you decided _____ a date for your wedding yet?

8. Patricia applied _____ admission _____ the university.

9. Daniel dreamed _____ some of his childhood friends last night.

10. Mr. Miyagi dreams _____ owning his own business someday.

11. The accused woman was innocent _____ the crime with which she was charged.

12. Ms. Sanders is friendly _____ everyone.

13. The secretary provided me _____ a great deal of information.

14. Ivan compared the wedding customs in his country _____ those in the United States.

▶ Practice 26. The subjunctive in noun clauses. (Chart F)

Complete the sentences with appropriate verbs. There is often more than one possible completion.

1. Mr. Adams insists that we _____*be*_____ careful in our writing.

2. They requested that we not _____ after midnight.

3. She demanded that I _____ her the truth.

4. I recommended that Rita _____ to the head of the department.

5. I suggest that everyone _____ a letter to the governor.

6. It is essential that I _____ you tomorrow.

7. It is important that he _____ the director of the English program.

8. It is necessary that everyone _____ here on time.

► **Practice 27. The subjunctive in noun clauses.** (Chart F)
Complete each sentence with the correct form of the verb in parentheses. Some of the verbs are passive.

1. Her advisor recommended that she (*take*) ____take____ five courses.

2. Roberto insisted that the new baby (*name*) _be named_ after his grandfather.

3. The doctor recommended that she (*stay*) _____ in bed for a few days.

4. The students requested that the test (*postpone*) _____, but the instructor decided against a postponement.

5. It is essential that no one (*admit*) _____ to the room without proper identification.

6. It is critical that pollution (*control*) _____ and eventually (*eliminate*) _____ .

7. It was such a beautiful day that one of the students suggested we (*have*) _____ class outside.

8. The movie director insisted that everything about his productions (*be*) _____ authentic.

9. It is vital that no one else (*know*) _____ about the secret government operation.

10. Mrs. Wah asked that we (*be*) _____ sure to lock the door behind us.

11. I requested that I (*permit*) _____ to change my class.

12. It is important that you (*be, not*) _____ late.

13. It is imperative that he (*return*) _____ home immediately.

14. The governor proposed that a new highway (*build*) _____ .

15. Fumiko specifically asked that I (*tell, not*) _____ anyone else about it.

16. She said it was important that no one else (*tell*) _____ about it.

▶ **Practice 28. Troublesome verbs.** (Chart G)
Choose the correct verb in parentheses.

1. The student (*raised* / *rose*) his hand in class.

2. Hot air (*raises* / *rises*).

3. Natasha (*set* / *sat*) in a chair because she was tired.

4. I (*set* / *sat*) your dictionary on the table a few minutes ago.

5. Hens (*lay* / *lie*) eggs.

6. Sara is (*laying* / *lying*) on the grass in the park right now.

7. Jan (*laid* / *lay*) the comb on top of the dresser a few minutes ago.

8. If you are tired, you should (*lay* / *lie*) down and take a nap.

9. San Francisco (*lays* / *lies*) to the north of Los Angeles.

10. Mr. Faust (*raises* / *rises*) many different kinds of flowers in his garden.

11. The student (*raised* / *rose*) from her seat and walked to the front of the auditorium to receive her diploma.

12. Hiroki is a very methodical person. Every night before going to bed, he (*lays* / *lies*) his clothes for the next day on his chair.

13. Where are my keys? I (*lay* / *laid*) them here on the desk five minutes ago.

14. Fahad (*set* / *sat*) the table for dinner.

15. Fahad (*set* / *sat*) at the table for dinner.

16. The fulfillment of all your dreams (*lies* / *lays*) within you — if you just believe in yourself.

Special Workbook Section
Phrasal Verbs

PHRASAL VERBS (TWO-WORD AND THREE-WORD VERBS)

The term *phrasal verb* refers to a verb and particle which together have a special meaning. For example, ***put + off*** means "postpone." Sometimes a phrasal verb consists of three parts. For example, ***put + up + with*** means "tolerate." Phrasal verbs are also called *two-word verbs* or *three-word verbs*.

SEPARABLE PHRASAL VERBS	A phrasal verb may be either *separable* or *nonseparable*. With a separable phrasal verb, a noun may come either between the verb and the preposition or after the preposition, as in (a) and (b). A pronoun comes between the verb and the preposition if the phrasal verb is separable, as in (c).
(a) ***I handed*** my paper ***in*** yesterday. (b) ***I handed in*** my paper yesterday. (c) ***I handed*** it ***in*** yesterday. (INCORRECT: I handed in it yesterday.)	
NONSEPARABLE PHRASAL VERBS	With a nonseparable phrasal verb, a noun or pronoun must follow the preposition, as in (d) and (e).
(d) ***I ran into*** an old friend yesterday. (e) ***I ran into*** her yesterday. (INCORRECT: I ran an old friend into.) (INCORRECT: I ran her into yesterday.)	

Phrasal verbs are especially common in informal English. Following is a list of common phrasal verbs and their usual meanings. This list contains only those phrasal verbs used in the exercises in the text. The phrasal verbs marked with an asterisk (*) are nonseparable.

A ask out . . . . *ask someone to go on a date*

B bring about, bring on . . . . *cause*
  bring up . . . . *(1) rear children; (2) mention or introduce a topic*

C call back . . . . *return a telephone call*
  call in . . . . *ask to come to an official place for a specific purpose*
  call off . . . . *cancel*
  *call on . . . . *ask to speak in class*
  call up . . . . *call on the telephone*
  *catch up (with). . . . . *reach the same position or level*
  *check in, check into . . . . *register at a hotel*
  check into . . . . *investigate*
  check out . . . . *(1) borrow a book from the library; (2) investigate*
  check out (of) . . . . *leave a hotel*
  cheer up . . . . *make (someone) feel happier*
  clean up . . . . *make clean and orderly*
  *come across . . . . *meet / find by chance*
  cross out . . . . *draw a line through*
  cut out . . . . *stop an annoying activity*

D do over. *do again*
  *drop by, drop in (on). . . . . *visit informally*
  drop off . . . . *leave something / someone at a place*
  *drop out (of) . . . . *stop going to school, to a class, to a club, etc.*

F	figure out	*find the answer by reasoning*
	fill out	*write the answers to a questionnaire or complete an official form*
	find out	*discover information*
G	*get along (with)	*have a good relationship with*
	get back (from)	*(1) return from a place; (2) receive again*
	*get in, get into	*(1) enter a car; (2) arrive*
	*get off	*leave an airplane, a bus, a train, a subway, a bicycle*
	*get on	*enter an airplane, a bus, a train, a subway, a bicycle*
	*get out of.	*(1) leave a car; (2) avoid work or an unpleasant activity*
	get over	*recover from an illness*
	get through (with)	*finish*
	*get up (from).	*arise from a bed, a chair*
	give back.	*return an item to someone*
	give up	*stop trying, quit*
	*go over	*review or check carefully*
	*grow up	*become an adult*
H	hand in.	*submit an assignment*
	hang up	*(1) conclude a telephone conversation; (2) put clothes on a hanger or a hook*
	have on	*wear*
K	keep out (of)	*not enter*
	*keep up (with)	*stay at the same position or level*
	kick out (of)	*force (someone) to leave*
L	*look after.	*take care of*
	*look into	*investigate*
	*look out (for).	*be careful*
	look over	*review or check carefully*
	look up.	*look for information in a reference book, on the internet, etc.*
M	make up	*(1) invent; (2) do past-due work*
N	name after, name for.	*give a baby the name of someone else*
P	*pass away, pass on	*die*
	pass out	*distribute*
	*pass out	*lose consciousness*
	pick out	*select*
	pick up.	*(1) go to get someone (e.g., in a car); (2) take in one's hand*
	point out.	*call attention to*
	put away	*remove to a proper place*
	put back	*return to the original place*
	put off	*postpone*
	put on	*put clothes on one's body*
	put out.	*extinguish a cigarette, cigar, fire*
	*put up with	*tolerate*
R	*run into, *run across.	*meet by chance*
	*run out (of)	*finish a supply of something*
S	*show up	*appear, come*
	shut off.	*stop a machine, light, faucet*

T *take after . . . . *resemble*
take off . . . . *(1) remove clothing; (2) leave on a trip*
take out . . . . *(1) take someone on a date; (2) remove*
take over . . . . *take control*
take up . . . . *begin a new activity or topic*
tear down . . . . *demolish; reduce to nothing*
tear up . . . . *tear into many little pieces*
think over . . . . *consider carefully*
throw away, throw out . . . . *discard, get rid of*
throw up . . . . *vomit; regurgitate food*
try on . . . . *put on clothing to see if it fits*
turn down . . . . *decrease volume or intensity*
turn in . . . . *(1) submit an assignment; (2) go to bed*
turn off . . . . *stop a machine, light, faucet*
turn on . . . . *start a machine, light, faucet*
turn out . . . . *extinguish a light*
turn up . . . . *increase volume or intensity*

▶ Practice 1. Phrasal verbs.

Complete each sentence with the appropriate preposition(s). The meaning of the phrasal verb is in parentheses.

1. Lara looked . . .

    a. ___*after*___ her father when he was sick. (*took care of*)

    b. _____ her children's homework. (*reviewed*)

    c. _____ some information on the internet. (*looked for information*)

    d. _____ an unusual situation at work. (*investigated*)

2. The tourists checked . . .

    a. _____ travel DVDs from the library before their trip. (*borrowed*)

    b. _____ their hotel. (*registered at*)

    c. _____ a famous archeological site. (*investigated*)

    d. _____ _____ their hotel rooms. (*left*)

3. Mrs. Jenkins got . . .

    a. _____ a serious illness. (*recovered from*)

    b. _____ _____ her planning for her daughter's wedding. (*finished*)

    c. _____ _____ doing an unimportant project at work. (*avoided*)

    d. _____ _____ her summer vacation early. (*returned*)

    e. _____ the subway at an unfamiliar stop. (*left*)

4. The school principal called . . .

   a. _____ the school assembly. (*canceled*)

   b. _____ some parents. (*telephoned*)

   c. _____ a few students to answer questions while visiting a class. (*asked them to speak*)

   d. _____ a teacher who was sick. (*returned a phone call*)

   e. _____ a student for discipline. (*asked the student to come to his/her office*)

▶ **Practice 2. Phrasal verbs.**

Complete each sentence with the correct form of a phrasal verb from the list. One phrasal verb is used twice.

get along with	pass out (2)	put up with	take after	turn in
pass away	pick out	show up	think over	

1. The flight attendants gave one snack to passengers during the flight. They _passed_ _out_ small bags of peanuts.

2. You choose the vegetables for dinner. _____ _____ whatever you like.

3. You look like your mother, but your brother _____ _____ your father.

4. I have three good job offers to consider. I need some time to _____ them _____ .

5. Nathan tolerates his roommate's messy habits. I wonder how he _____ _____ _____ them.

6. Mary's elderly mother died last week. She _____ _____ after a long illness.

7. Julianna was two hours late for the dinner party. When she finally appeared, her friends told her it was rude to _____ _____ so late.

8. The Smiths are a friendly couple and people really like them. They seem to _____ _____ _____ everyone.

9. Good night. It's bedtime. I'm going to _____ _____ now.

10. Helen got hit in the head with a golf ball, but fortunately didn't lose consciousness. The ball was traveling so fast that it was a miracle she didn't _____ _____ .

▶ Practice 3. Phrasal verbs.

Choose the correct completions. More than one completion may be correct.

1. When do we turn in   (our assignment?)   the dinner?   yesterday?

2. Mario made up   a lie.   a story.   a flower.

3. The government took over   the city.   the banks.   the trees.

4. Please put out   your cigarette.   the lights.   the fire.

5. What brought about   the war?   the package?   the crisis?

6. Did you figure out   working?   the problem?   the puzzle?

7. How do I turn on   the lights?   the music?   the printer?

8. Hugo asked out   his classmate.   a question.   a girl.

9. Jill is going to give up   a present.   chocolate.   smoking.

10. At the airport, I came across a friend.   a classmate.   to fly.

11. Tina dropped out of   high school.   the ball.   college.

▶ Practice 4. Phrasal verbs.

Complete each sentence with an appropriate preposition from the list to form a two-word verb. Some prepositions may be used more than once.

| back | into | off | on | out | up |

1. A: Guess who I ran ____into____ today as I was walking across campus. Ann Keefe!

   B: You're kidding!

2. A: There will be a test on Chapters 8 and 9 next Friday.

   B: Oh, no! Couldn't you put it _____ until Monday?

3. A: You'd better put _____ your coat before you leave. It's chilly out.

   B: What's the temperature?

4. A: I smell something burning in the kitchen. Can I call you _____ in a minute?

   B: Sure. I hope your dinner hasn't burned.

   A: So do I! Bye.

5. A: I think that if I learn enough vocabulary I won't have any trouble using English.

   B: That's not necessarily so. I'd like to point _____ that language consists of much more than just vocabulary.

6. A: Your children certainly love the outdoors.

   B: Yes, they do. We brought them _____ to appreciate nature.

7. A: What forms do I have to fill out to change my tourist visa to a student visa?

   B: I don't know, but I'll look _____ it first thing tomorrow and try to find _____. I'll let you know.

8. A: How long were you in the hospital?

   B: About a week. But I've missed almost two weeks of classes.

   A: It's going to be hard for you to make _____ all the work you've missed, isn't it?

   B: Very.

9. A: Could you pick _____ a newspaper on your way home from work tonight? There's a story I want to read.

   B: Sure.

10. A: I like your new shoes.

    B: Thanks. I had to try _____ almost a dozen pairs before I decided to get these.

▶ **Practice 5. Phrasal verbs.**
Complete each sentence with an appropriate preposition from the list to form a two-word verb. Some prepositions may be used more than once.

about	away	in	of	off	on	out	up

1. A: I'm trying to find yesterday's newspaper. Have you seen it?

   B: I'm afraid I threw it _____*away / out*_____. I thought you had finished reading it.

2. A: Where did you grow _____?

   B: In Seattle, Washington.

3. A: Don't forget to turn the lights _____ before you go to bed.

   B: I won't.

4.　A: I have a car, so I can drive us to the festival.

　　B: Good.

　　A: What time should I pick you _____?

　　B: Any time after five would be fine.

5.　A: We couldn't see the show at the outdoor theater last night.

　　B: Why not?

　　A: It was called _____ on account of rain.

6.　A: Thomas looks sad.

　　B: I think he misses his girlfriend.　Let's try to cheer him _____ .

7.　A: What brought _____ your decision to quit your present job?

　　B: I was offered a better job.

8.　A: Why did you come back early from your trip?

　　B: Unfortunately, I ran _____ _____ money.

9.　A: Thanks for the ride.　I appreciate it.

　　B: Where should I drop you _____?

10.　A: What time does your plane take _____?

　　B: 10:40.

　　A: How long does the flight take?

　　B: I think we get _____ around 12:30.

▶ Practice 6. Phrasal verbs.
Complete the sentences with appropriate prepositions to form two-word or three-word verbs.

1.　A: Look __*out*__! A car is coming!

2.　A: May I borrow your dictionary?

　　B: Sure.　But please be sure to put it _____ on the shelf when you're finished.

3.　A: I'm going to be in your neighborhood tomorrow.

　　B: Oh?　If you have time, why don't you drop _____ to see us?

4. A: How does this tape recorder work?

   B: Push this button to turn it _____ and push that button to shut it

   _____ .

5. A: Did you hear what started the forest fire?

   B: Yes. Some campers built a fire, but when they left their campsite, they didn't

   _____ it _____ completely.

6. A: I need to talk to Karen.

   B: Why don't you call her _____ ? She's probably at home now.

7. A: Uh-oh. I made a mistake on the check I just wrote.

   B: Don't try to correct the mistake. Just tear _____ the check and throw it

   _____ .

8. A: Are you here to apply for a job?

   B: Yes.

   A: Here is an application form. Fill it _____ and then give it _____ to

   me when you are finished.

9. A: Look. There's Mike.

   B: Where?

   A: At the other end of the block, walking toward the administration building. If we run, we

   can catch _____ with him.

10. A: Is your roommate here?

    B: Yes. She decided to come to the party after all. Have you ever met her?

    A: No, but I'd like to.

    B: She's the one standing over there by the far window. She has a blue dress

    _____ . Come on. I'll introduce you.

▶ Practice 7. Phrasal verbs.

Complete each sentence with an appropriate preposition.

1. A: What time did you get _____*up*_____ this morning?

    B: I slept late. I didn't drag myself out of bed until after nine.

2. A: How did you do on your composition?

    B: Not well. It had a lot of spelling mistakes, so I have to do it _____ .

3. A: What's the baby's name?

    B: Helen. She was named _____ her paternal grandmother.

4. A: I need to get more exercise.

    B: Why don't you take _____ tennis?

5. A: You can't go in there.

    B: Why not?

    A: Look at that sign. It says, "Keep _____ . No trespassing."

6. A: The radio is too loud. Would you mind if I turned it _____ a little?

    B: No.

7. A: I can't hear the radio. Could you turn it _____ a little?

    B: Sure.

8. A: What are you doing Saturday night, Bob?

    B: I'm taking Virginia _____ for dinner and a show.

9. A: Don't you think it's hot in here?

    B: Not especially. If you're hot, why don't you take your sweater _____ ?

10. A: How do you spell *occasionally*?

    B: I'm not sure. You'd better look it _____ in your dictionary.

11. A: I'm tired. I wish I could get _____ of going to the meeting tonight.

    B: Why do you have to go?

▶ Practice 8. Phrasal verbs.

Complete each sentence with an appropriate preposition.

1. A: I need my dictionary, but I lent it to José.

   B: Why don't you get it _____*back*_____ from him?

2. A: Cindy is only three. She likes to play with the older kids, but when they're running and playing, she can't keep _____ with them.

   B: She doesn't seem to mind, does she?

3. A: I made a mistake in my composition. What should I do?

   B: Since it's an in-class composition, just cross it _____ .

4. A: What happened when the pilot of the plane passed out during the flight?

   B: The co-pilot took _____ .

5. I took a plane from Atlanta to Miami. I got _____ the plane in Atlanta. I got _____ the plane in Miami.

6. It was a snowy winter day, but I still had to drive to work. First I got _____ the car to start the engine. Then I got _____ of the car to scrape the snow and ice from the windows.

7. Last year I took a train trip. I got _____ the train in Chicago. I got _____ the train in Des Moines.

8. Phyllis takes the bus to work. She gets _____ the bus at Lindbergh Boulevard and gets _____ the bus about two blocks from her office on Tower Street.

9. A: Do you like living in the dorm?

   B: It's OK. I've learned to put _____ _____ all the noise.

10. A: What brought _____ your decision to quit your job?

    B: I couldn't get _____ _____ my boss.

11. A: Did you go _____ your paper carefully before you handed it _____ ?

    B: Yes. I looked it _____ carefully.

Index

Answer Key

CHAPTER 12: NOUN CLAUSES

PRACTICE 1, p. 117
Noun Clauses
1. what he said
2. None
3. what happened
4. None
5. why Dora is calling me
6. who that man is
7. where Hank lives
8. None
9. What they are doing
10. None
11. what I should say
12. None

PRACTICE 2, p. 117
1. do they want
2. what they want
3. does Stacy live
4. where Stacy lives
5. what Carl likes
6. does Carl like
7. is Lina going
8. where Lina is going

PRACTICE 3, p. 118
1. Where does Lee Live? **D**oes he live downtown?
2. I don't know <u>where he lives</u>.
3. What does Sandra want? **D**o you know?
4. Do you know <u>what Sandra wants</u>?
5. <u>What Yoko knows</u> is important to us.
6. We talked about <u>what Yoko knows</u>.
7. What do you think? **D**id you tell your professor <u>what you think</u>?
8. My professor knows <u>what I think</u>.
9. Where is the bus stop? **D**o you know where the bus stop is?
10. What did he report? <u>What he reported</u> is important.

PRACTICE 4, p. 118
1. how far it is
2. what that is on the table
3. how much it cost
4. What he said
5. when they are leaving
6. which road we should take
7. who called
8. what's happening
9. why they work at night

10. What they are trying to do
11. what kind of insects these are
12. whose keys these are

PRACTICE 5, p. 118
1. Who is that man?
   Noun clause: who that man is.
2. Where does George live?
   Noun clause: where George lives.
3. What did Ann buy?
   Noun clause: what Ann bought?
4. How far is it to Denver from here?
   Noun clause: how far it is to Denver from here.
5. Why was Jack late for class?
   Noun clause: why Jack was late for class.
6. Whose pen is that?
   Noun clause: whose pen that is.
7. Who did Alex see at the meeting?
   Noun clause: who Alex saw at the meeting.
8. Who saw Ms. Frost at the meeting?
   Noun clause: who saw Ms. Frost at the meeting?
9. Which book does Alice like best?
   Noun clause: which book Alice likes best.
10. What time is the plane supposed to land?
    Noun clause: what time the plane is supposed to land?

PRACTICE 6, p. 119
1. b	4. a	6. d
2. c	5. f	7. g, h
3. e		

PRACTICE 7, p. 120
1. a, b, c, d, f
2. a, b
3. b, e

PRACTICE 8, p. 120
1. how much this book costs?
2. when Flight 62 is expected?
3. where the nearest phone is?
4. if this word is spelled correctly?
5. what time it is?
6. if this information is correct?
7. how much it costs to fly from Toronto to London?
8. where the bus station is?
9. whose pen this is?
10. if this bus goes downtown?

PRACTICE 9, p. 121
1. g	3. e	5. f	7. d
2. a	4. c	6. b	8. h

PRACTICE 10, p. 121

1. proud
2. angry
3. disappointed
4. aware
5. lucky
6. confident
7. worried . . . relieved

PRACTICE 11, p. 122

1. a. It is surprising that . . . .
   b. . . . nobody stopped to help Sam . . . is surprising
2. a. It is unfortunate that . . .
   b. That people in modern cities are . . . is unfortunate
3. a. It is still true that people . . . .
   b. That people in my village . . . help . . . . is still true.
4. a. It is undeniably true that . . .
   b. That people need each other . . . is undeniably true
5. a. It seems strange to . . . that people in cities live
   b. The fact that people in cities . . . don't know their neighbors

PRACTICE 12, p. 122

1. Millie said, "There's an important meeting at 3:00 o'clock today."
2. "There's an important meeting at 3:00 o'clock today," she said.
3. "There is," said Millie, "an important meeting at 3:00 o'clock today."
4. "There is an important meeting today. It's about the new rules," said Millie.
5. "Where is the meeting?" Carl asked.
6. Robert replied, "It's in the conference room."
7. "How long will it last?" asked Ali.
8. "I don't know how long it will last," replied Millie.
9. "I'll be a little late," said Robert. "I have another meeting until 3:00 P.M. today."
10. "Who is speaking at the meeting?" asked Robert.
11. "I am not sure who is speaking," said Millie, "but you'd better be there. Everybody is supposed to be there."

PRACTICE 13, p. 123

(1) "You are so slow, Mr. Turtle," said the rabbit, "and I am very fast."
(2) "I don't know about that," said the turtle. "Let's have a race. We will run for five miles and see who wins."
(3) "I agree," said the rabbit.
(4) "I am so far ahead of the turtle. I am going to take a little nap right here. It is going to take a long time before that turtle can catch up with me."
(5) The turtle looked back at the rabbit and exclaimed, "Slow but steady wins the race. Who's laughing now, Mr. Rabbit?"

PRACTICE 14, p. 123

1. was
2. needed
3. was having
4. had finished
5. had finished
6. would arrive
7. was going to be
8. could solve
9. might come
10. might come
11. had to leave
12. had to leave
13. should go
14. to stay

PRACTICE 15, p. 124

1. if / whether she was planning
2. what time the movie begins
3. if / whether we could still get
4. how he can help
5. if / whether he could help
6. when the final decision would be made
7. where she had been
8. what Kim's native language is
9. if / whether I was doing
10. what time he had
11. who she should give this message
12. why I hadn't called

PRACTICE 16, p. 125

Conversation 1.

1. was going
2. was
3. asked
4. would like
5. had
6. had
7. was
8. could
9. were

Conversation 2.

1. asked
2. was
3. told
4. was
5. said
6. was
7. had heard
8. had
9. was
10. had been
11. asked
12. had been
13. had not
14. told
15. had gone
16. was

PRACTICE 17, p. 126

1. whenever
2. wherever
3. whatever
4. however
5. whichever
6. whomever
7. whichever
8. whoever
9. whatever
10. wherever

CHAPTER 13: ADJECTIVE CLAUSES

PRACTICE 1, p. 127

1. person — who fixes computers
2. man — who lives on a boat
3. woman — who speaks four languages
4. people — who are bilingual in the office
5. office — that is in an old building
6. building — which we work in
7. trees — that were over two hundred years old
8. trees — which were nearby
9. truck — that had broken down
10. truck — which caused the problem

PRACTICE 2, p. 127

1. a, b
2. a, b
3. c, d
4. a, b
5. b, c
6. b, c

PRACTICE 3, p. 128

Adjective Clauses

1. man — that I met last night
2. woman — that Sandro is going to marry
3. people — whom we invited
4. book — which I just read
5. program — that Jason installed
6. house — we built in 1987
7. cake — I left on the table
8. book — my professor wrote

PRACTICE 4, p. 128

1. a, b, c, f
2. a, c, e, f
3. c, d, e
4. a, b, c, e
5. a, c, d, e
6. a, b, c, f

PRACTICE 5, p. 128

1. . . . I read was good
2. . . . I saw was very sad
3. . . . can live a long time
4. . . . we photographed
5. . . . does many things at the same time
6. . . . can trust
7. . . . the thieves stole was valuable

PRACTICE 6, p. 129

1. c, d, g, i
2. a, b, f, h

PRACTICE 7, p. 129

1. that / who / whom / Ø
2. who / that
3. that / which / Ø
4. which
5. that / who / Ø
6. who / that
7. whom
8. that / which

PRACTICE 8, p. 130

1. ~~it~~
2. ~~he~~
3. ~~it~~
4. ~~to~~
5. for ~~who~~ whom
6. ~~who~~ that which
7. People **who** have
8. ~~him~~
9. ~~she~~
10. ~~which~~ who / that

PRACTICE 9, p. 130

1. b   5. b
2. a   6. b
3. b   7. a, c
4. a

PRACTICE 10, p. 131

1. **His** refers to **man**.
   Do you know the man whose car is parked over there?
2. **His** refers to **doctor**.
   I know a skin doctor whose name is Dr. Skinner.
3. **Their** refers to **people**.
   The people whose home we visited were very hospitable.
4. **Her** refers to **Mrs. Lake**.
   Mrs. Lake is the teacher whose class I enjoy the most.
5. **Their** refers to **parents**.
   The teacher asked the parents whose children were failing to confer with her.

PRACTICE 11, p. 131

1. b, c   5. a, b
2. a, c   6. b
3. c   7. a, c
4. a, c

PRACTICE 12, p. 132

1. a. where I grew up   b. in which I grew up
2. a. I lived in   b. where I lived
3. a. where I lived   b. on which I lived
4. a. where I played   b. in which I played

PRACTICE 13, p. 132

1. a. that I go
   b. on which I go
   c. when I go
2. a. when I play tennis
   b. that I play tennis
   c. on which I play tennis

PRACTICE 14, p. 133

1. e
2. c
3. f
4. d
5. a
6. h
7. g
8. b

PRACTICE 15, p. 133

1. a, d
2. b
3. c, d
4. a, b, c
5. d
6. b, c
7. c, d
8. a

PRACTICE 16, p. 134

1. c
2. h
3. a
4. f
5. g
6. b
7. e
8. d

PRACTICE 17, p. 134

1. no
2. yes   I made an appointment with Dr. Raven, who is an expert on eye disorders.
3. yes   Bogota, which is the capital of Columbia, is a cosmopolitan city.
4. no
5. yes   South Beach, which is clean, pleasant, and fun, is known as a party town.
6. yes   The name Bogota comes from the word *Bacata*, which was the Indian name for the site.
7. no
8. yes   . . . Belinda Jones, who wrote a touching essay . . .
9. yes   . . . Nairobi, which is near several fascinating game reserves, . . .
10. no
11. no
12. no
13. no
14. yes   A typhoon, which is a violent tropical storm, can cause . . .
15. no
16. yes   Hurricane Katrina, which destroyed parts of New Orleans, occurred in 2005.

PRACTICE 18, p. 135

1. a   3. a   5. b   7. b
2. b   4. b   6. a   8. a

PRACTICE 19, p. 136

1. I received two job offers, neither of which I accepted.
2. I have three brothers, two of whom are professional athletes.
3. Jerry is engaged in several business ventures, only one of which is profitable.
4. The two women, both of whom began their studies at age 40, have almost completed law school.
5. Eric is proud of his success, much of which has been due to hard work, but some of which has been due to good luck.
6. We ordered an extra-large pizza, half of which contained meat and half of which didn't.
7. The scientist won the Nobel Prize for his groundbreaking work, most of which was on genomes.
8. The audience gave a tremendous ovation to the Nobel prize winners, most of whom were scientists.

PRACTICE 20, p. 136

1. Mike was accepted at the state university, which is surprising.
2. Mike did not do well in high school, which is unfortunate.
3. The university accepts a few students each year with a low grade-point average, which is lucky for Mike.
4. The university hopes to motivate these low-performing students, which is a fine idea.
5. Mike might actually be a college graduate one day, which would be a miracle!

PRACTICE 21, p. 137

1. ~~who is wearing a green hat~~   wearing a green hat
2. ~~who is in charge of this department~~   in charge of this department
3. ~~which was painted by Picasso~~   painted

4. ~~who are doing research~~   doing research
5. ~~which are in progress~~   in progress
6. ~~which are scheduled to begin in September~~   scheduled to begin in September
7. ~~which is the largest city in Canada~~   the largest city in Canada
8. ~~that orbit the sun~~   orbiting the sun
9. ~~which was formerly known as a planet~~   formerly known as a planet
10. ~~which means to "devalue someone or something"~~   meaning to "devalue someone or something"

PRACTICE 22, p. 137

1. Brasilia, **officially inaugurated in 1960,** is the capital of Brazil. ~~It was officially inaugurated in 1960.~~
2. Rio de Janeiro, **the second largest city in Brazil,** used to be its capital. ~~It is the second largest city in Brazil.~~
3. Two languages, Finnish and Swedish, are spoken in Helsinki, **the capital of Finland.** ~~It is the capital of Finland.~~
4. In Canada, you see signs, **written in both English and French.** ~~They are written in both English and French.~~
5. Libya, **a country in North Africa,** is a leading producer of oil. ~~It is a country in North Africa.~~
6. Simon Bolivar, **a great South American general,** led the fight for independence in the nineteenth century. ~~He was a great South American general.~~
7. Five South American countries, **liberated by Bolivar,** are Venezuela, Colombia, Ecuador, Panama, and Peru. ~~They were liberated by Bolivar.~~
8. We need someone, **holding a degree in electrical engineering,** to design this project. ~~He or she holds a degree in electrical engineering.~~
9. The project **being built in Beijing** will be finished next year. ~~It is being built in Beijing.~~
10. A lot of new buildings were constructed in Beijing in 2008, **the site of the summer Olympics that year.** ~~Beijing was the site of the summer Olympics in that year.~~

PRACTICE 23, p. 138

Sample answers:

1. . . . a lot of people **waiting** in . . .
2. Students **who are** living on . . . OR Students **living** on . . .
3. . . . the librarian **who sits** . . . OR the librarian **sitting** . . .
4. . . . Anna **whose** birthday . . .
5. . . . Sapporo, **which** is . . .
6. Patrick, who is my oldest brother, is married and has one child.
7. The person **sitting** next to me is someone I've never **met.**
8. . . . is a small **city located** on . . .
9. . . . person to **whom** I wanted . . .
10. There are eighty **students from** all over the world **studying** English at this school.
11. The people who we **met on** our trip last May . . .
12. Dianne Baxter, **who** used to teach Spanish, has organized . . .
13. . . . since I came here, **some of whom** are from my country.
14. People **who** can speak English . . .
15. Grandpa is getting married again, **which** is a big surprise.

CHAPTER 14: GERUNDS AND INFINITIVES, PART 1

PRACTICE 1, p. 139

Gerunds:
1. Driving
2. driving
3. None
4. singing
5. Singing
6. None

PRACTICE 2, p. 139

1. taking
2. going
3. improving
4. flying
5. lowering
6. buying
7. drinking
8. hearing

PRACTICE 3, p. 140

Part I.
1. in
2. of
3. of
4. for
5. from

Part II.
6. of
7. for
8. to
9. to
10. of

PRACTICE 4, p. 140

1. b
2. b
3. c
4. c
5. a
6. c
7. a
8. c
9. c
10. b

PRACTICE 5, p. 141

1. about leaving
2. for being
3. from completing
4. about having
5. of studying
6. for not wanting
7. for washing . . . drying
8. of stealing
9. to eating . . . sleeping
10. for lending

PRACTICE 6, p. 141

1. about taking
2. in buying
3. to living
4. for not answering
5. about failing
6. about changing
7. for cleaning
8. from arriving
9. for writing
10. in saving . . . from wasting

PRACTICE 7, p. 142

1. playing
2. smoking
3. driving
4. paying
5. arguing
6. selling
7. having
8. reading

PRACTICE 8, p. 142

Part I.
1. go hiking
2. go sailing
3. go skiing
4. went birdwatching
5. went canoeing

Part II.
6. go dancing
7. go bowling
8. will go sightseeing
9. will go window shopping

PRACTICE 9, p. 143

1. playing
2. lying
3. locating
4. looking
5. doing
6. watching

PRACTICE 10, p. 144

1. a, c
2. a
3. a, c
4. c
5. a
6. a, c

PRACTICE 11, p. 144

1. to work
2. me to work
3. to work
4. to work / me to work
5. to work
6. to work
7. to work
8. me to work
9. me to work
10. to work / me to work
11. to work / me to work
12. to work
13. to work / me to work
14. me to work

PRACTICE 12, p. 144

1. permitted me to leave early
2. asked me to give this note to Sue
3. advised me to take Biology 109
4. ordered me to pay a fine
5. warned Greg to keep his eyes on his own paper
6. warned Greg not to look at his neighbor's paper
7. told the children to be quiet
8. allowed me to stay up late on Saturday night
9. encouraged the students to speak slowly and clearly
10. expects the students to come to class on time

PRACTICE 13, p. 145

1. The teacher allowed the children to go outside and play.
   The children were allowed to go outside and play.
2. The doctor warned my father not to eat high-cholesterol foods.
   My father was warned not to eat high-cholesterol foods.
3. The sergeant ordered the soldiers to march in formation.
   The soldiers were ordered to march in formation.
4. The soccer coach encouraged the girls to play hard and win.
   The girls were encouraged to play hard and win.
5. Mary reminded her roommate to wake her up at 7:00.
   Mary's roommate was reminded to wake her up at 7:00.
6. The police officer permitted the drivers in our lane of traffic to go ahead.
   The drivers in our lane of traffic were permitted to go ahead.
7. The letter told me to complete this form by November 15th.
   I was told to complete this form by November 15th.

PRACTICE 14, p. 145

1. a	7. a
2. a	8. a
3. b	9. b
4. b	10. a
5. b	11. a
6. b	12. b

PRACTICE 15, p. 146

1. living	8. exercising
2. to be	9. me to exercise
3. to show	10. to exercise
4. making	11. to exercise
5. to be	12. my friend to consult
6. being	13. to consult
7. humming	14. to recommend

PRACTICE 16, p. 147

Part I.

1. to stay	6. him to stay
2. to stay	7. to stay
3. him to stay	8. to stay
4. him to stay	9. him to stay
5. staying	10. to stay

Part II.

1. traveling	6. traveling
2. traveling	7. traveling
3. to travel	8. traveling
4. traveling	9. traveling
5. to travel	10. traveling

Part III.

1. working	6. working
2. to work	7. him to work
3. to work	8. to work
4. to work	9. to work
5. to work	10. working

PRACTICE 17, p. 147

1. to turn	7. speaking
2. meeting	8. buying
3. to stop	9. to tell
4. seeing	10. to learn
5. telling	11. talking
6. to talk	

PRACTICE 18, p. 148

1. b	4. a
2. a	5. b
3. b	

PRACTICE 19, p. 148

1. a, b
2. a
3. a, b
4. a
5. a, b
6. a, b
7. a, b
8. b
9. b
10. a, b

PRACTICE 20, p. 149

1. It's	6. It's
2. is	7. is
3. is not	8. to jump
4. Is it	9. To see
5. Going	10. Is

PRACTICE 21, p. 149

1. a, b, d, g, i, k, l
2. a, d, f, h, j, k, l

PRACTICE 22, p. 150

1. b	8. b
2. a	9. a
3. b	10. a
4. b	11. b
5. a	12. a
6. a	13. a
7. b	14. b

PRACTICE 23, p. 151

1. camping	7. reading
2. to operate	8. to end
3. getting	9. using . . . speaking
4. applying	10. watching
5. to turn	11. running
6. sleeping	

PRACTICE 24, p. 152

1. . . . enjoy **watching** . . .
2. . . . spend time **playing** . . .
3. . . . important **to keep** . . .
4. . . . avoid **becoming** . . . by **exercising**
5. Playing word games **is** . . .
6. In addition, **it** is . . .
7. . . . people **to eat** . . .
8. . . . try **to eat** . . .
9. . . . interested **in learning** . . .
10. . . . wants **to live** . . .
11. . . . excited about **attending** . . .
12. . . . struggling **to learn** . . .
13. . . . hard time **pronouncing** . . .
14. He keeps on **studying** and **practicing**.
15. . . . in bed **listening** to . . .
16. . . . dreams **about / of** traveling . . .

CHAPTER 15: GERUNDS AND INFINITIVES, PART 2

PRACTICE 1, p. 153

1. ~~for~~ to	5. ~~for~~ to
2. Correct.	6. ~~to~~ for
3. Correct.	7. ~~for see~~ to see
4. Correct.	8. Correct.

PRACTICE 2, p. 153
1. a
2. a, b
3. a, b
4. a, b
5. a
6. a
7. a, b
8. a, b
9. a, b

PRACTICE 3, p. 154
1. d
2. c
3. b
4. a
5. f
6. e

PRACTICE 4, p. 154
1. very
2. too
3. too
4. too
5. very
6. very
7. very . . . too
8. too
9. too
10. very

PRACTICE 5, p. 155
1. very . . . enough
2. too
3. enough
4. very . . . enough
5. very . . . enough
6. too . . . enough
7. too . . . enough
8. very . . . enough
9. very
10. enough

PRACTICE 6, p. 155
1. to be accepted
2. to be given
3. to be picked
4. being petted
5. to be held
6. being invited
7. being noticed
8. being invited

PRACTICE 7, p. 155
1. b
2. a
3. b
4. b
5. a
6. b
7. a
8. b

PRACTICE 8, p. 156
1. b
2. a
3. b
4. b
5. a
6. b
7. b
8. a

PRACTICE 9, p. 156
1. to be called
2. being called
3. to be elected
4. to be elected
5. to be re-elected
6. being understood
7. to be left
8. to be loved . . . needed

PRACTICE 10, p. 157
1. a, c, d
2. a, c, d
3. a, c, d
4. a, c, d
5. a, c
6. b, c

PRACTICE 11, p. 157
1. practice / practicing
2. pass / passing
3. cry / crying
4. leave
5. win
6. arrive
7. rocking / rock
8. doing / do
9. talking / talk
10. reaching / reach

PRACTICE 12, p. 158
1. a
2. b
3. c
4. a, b
5. c
6. a
7. a, c
8. a

PRACTICE 13, p. 158
1. stand
2. fixed
3. beat
4. to stop
5. to clean
6. look
7. call
8. made . . . put

PRACTICE 14, p. 159
1. b
2. b, c
3. c
4. b
5. a
6. c
7. b, c
8. b
9. a

PRACTICE 15, p. 159
1. b
2. a
3. b
4. c
5. c
6. d
7. d
8. b
9. a
10. b
11. a
12. c
13. d
14. a
15. d

PRACTICE 16, p. 160
1. to buy
2. opening
3. being asked
4. having
5. to wear . . . dressing
6. jumping . . . falling
7. being taken
8. to stop delivering . . . to fill
9. gazing . . . to cheer
10. having

PRACTICE 17, p. 161
1. b
2. b
3. b
4. b
5. a
6. b
7. a
8. a
9. a
10. b
11. b
12. a
13. c
14. a
15. b
16. a
17. b
18. c
19. a
20. a
21. c

PRACTICE 18, p. 162

1.	~~playing~~	play
2.	~~to cry~~	crying
3.	~~take~~	taking
4.	~~being~~	to be
5.	~~signing~~	to sign
6.	~~to notify~~	notifying
7.	~~calling~~	call
8.	~~translated~~	to translate
9.	~~look~~	looking
10.	~~understanding~~	understand
11.	~~for~~	to
12.	~~to fish~~	fishing
13.	~~taking~~	to take
14.	~~eating~~	to eat
15.	~~eat~~	eating
16.	~~to burn~~	burning

CHAPTER 16: COORDINATING CONJUNCTIONS

PRACTICE 1, p. 163

1.	b	5.	c
2.	c	6.	c
3.	c	7.	a
4.	b	8.	b

PRACTICE 2, p. 163

1. Conjunction: and
   <u>sweet</u> and <u>fresh</u>   a. adjective
2. Conjunction: and
   <u>apples</u> and <u>pears</u>   b. noun
3. Conjunction: and
   <u>washed</u> and <u>dried</u>   c. verb
4. Conjunction: and
   <u>washing</u> and <u>drying</u>   c. verb
5. Conjunction: and
   <u>happily</u> and <u>quickly</u>   d. adverb
6. Conjunction: but
   <u>delicious</u> but <u>expensive</u>   a. adjective
7. Conjunction: and
   <u>Apples</u>, <u>pears</u>, and <u>bananas</u>   b. noun
8. Conjunction: or
   <u>apple</u> or a <u>banana</u>   b. noun
9. Conjunction: and
   <u>red</u>, <u>ripe</u>, and <u>juicy</u>   a. adjective

PRACTICE 3, p. 164

1. c
2. e
3. a
4. g
5. f
6. d
7. h
8. b

PRACTICE 4, p. 165

1. None.
2. calm, quiet, and serene.
3. the ball, and they ran. . . .
4. kicking, throwing, and running.
5. None.
6. sit down, be quiet, and open. . .
7. None.
8. None.
9. two cups of coffee, three glasses of water, one glass of orange juice, and three orders of eggs
10. strict, but fair OR strict but fair

PRACTICE 5, p. 165

1.	I	~~he is honest~~	, and honesty
2.	C		
3.	I	~~quiet~~	quietly
4.	C		
5.	C		
6.	I	~~to tour~~	touring
7.	C		
8.	I	~~summarizing~~	summarize
9.	C		
10.	C		
11.	I	~~they require~~	
12.	C		

PRACTICE 6, p. 166

1.	knows	7.	like
2.	know	8.	has
3.	knows	9.	agrees
4.	know	10.	are
5.	know	11.	realizes
6.	wants	12.	are

PRACTICE 7, p. 166

1. Both Mary and her parents drink coffee.
   Neither Mary nor her parents drink coffee.
2. Either John or Henry will do the work.
   Neither John nor Henry will do the work.
3. Not only our school but also the restaurants in town recycle trash.
   Both our school and the restaurants in town recycle trash.

PRACTICE 8, p. 166

Part I.
1. both her mother and her father
2. both the nurses and the doctor arrive
3. both bananas and mangos originated
4. both whales and dolphins are

Part II.
5. exports not only coffee but also oil
6. Not only Air Greenland but also Icelandair fly
7. not only a green jacket but also green pants
8. not only attended Harvard University but also Harvard Law School.

Part III.
9. Either Ricky or Paula knows
10. either to Mexico or Costa Rica
11. Either Jim or Taka's parents will take her
12. She's buying either salmon or tuna

13. neither Fred nor his children
14. neither she nor her children have
15. Luis has neither a family nor friends
16. neither hot nor cold

PRACTICE 9, p. 167

1. stopped. The birds . . .
2. stopped, and the birds . . .
3. stopped, . . . sang, ...
4. street. His mother . . .
5. street, and his mother . . . .
6. street. His mother . . . .
7. coffee, and
8. coffee. It is . . . .
9. ice cream, but . . . .

PRACTICE 10, p. 168

My brother is visiting me for a couple of days. We spent yesterday together in the city, and we had a really good time.

First I took him to the waterfront. We went to the aquarium. We saw fearsome sharks, some wonderfully funny marine mammals, and all kinds of tropical fish. After the aquarium, we went downtown to a big mall and went shopping.

I had trouble thinking of a place to take him for lunch because he's a strict vegetarian, but I remembered a restaurant that has vegan food. We went there, and we had a wonderful lunch of fresh vegetables and whole grains. I'm not a vegetarian, but I must say that I really enjoyed the meal.

In the afternoon, it started raining. We decided to go to a movie. It was pretty good but had too much violence for me. I felt tense when we left the theater. I prefer comedies or dramas. My brother loved the movie.

We ended the day with a delicious home-cooked meal and some good conversation in my living room. It was an excellent day. I like spending time with my brother.

PRACTICE 11, p. 168

1. John will call either Mary or Bob.
2. Sue saw not only the mouse but also the cat.
3. Both my mother and father talked to the teacher
4. . . . is going . . .
5. I enjoy reading not only novels but also magazines.
6. Both smallpox and malaria are dangerous diseases.
7. . . . compact car. She is saving . . . .
8. . . . snow tonight. The roads . . . .
9. . . . we attended an opera, ate at marvelous restaurants, and visited . . . .

PRACTICE 12, p. 169

Across	Down
3. but	1. Neither
4. only	2. Both
6. Either	3. and
7. nor	

CHAPTER 17: ADVERB CLAUSES

PRACTICE 1, p. 170

Adverb Clauses

1. as she was leaving the store
2. before we have breakfast
3. Since Douglas fell off his bicycle last week
4. Because I already had my boarding pass
5. if the workplace is made pleasant
6. After Ceylon had been independent for 24 years
7. as soon as she receives them
8. once he becomes familiar with the new computer program

PRACTICE 2, p. 170

1. . . . calm. Tom . . . .
2. . . . calm, Tom . . . .
3. . . . calm. He . . . .
4. . . . fishing, the lake was calm. He . . .
5. . . . calm, so Tom went fishing. He . . . .
6. . . . quiet, Tom . . . .
7. . . . calm, quiet, and clear . . . .
8. . . . poor, he . . . .
9. . . . poor. He . . . .
10. Microscopes, automobile dashboards, and cameras . . . people to use. They are designed . . . people. When "lefties" use these items, ...

PRACTICE 3, p. 171

1. b	7. b
2. c	8. c
3. d	9. b
4. c	10. a
5. c	11. d
6. d	12. a

PRACTICE 4, p. 171

1. 1, 2	5. 2, 1
2. 2, 1	6. 1, 2
3. 1, 2	7. S
4. 2, 1	8. 1, 2

PRACTICE 5, p. 172

1. d	6. j
2. i	7. c
3. a	8. e
4. f	9. b
5. h	10. g

PRACTICE 6, p. 172

1. My registration was cancelled because I didn't pay the registration fee on time.
2. I'm late because there was lot of traffic.
3. Because he was on a good weight-loss diet, Harry lost 35 pounds.
4. Since Mario's is closed on Sundays, we can't have lunch there tomorrow.
5. Now that Jack has a car, he drives to work.
6. Natalie should find another job since she is very unhappy in this job.
7. David will lead us because he knows the way.
8. Frank is looking for a job in a law office now that he has graduated from law school.

PRACTICE 7, p. 173

1. even though
2. because
3. Because
4. Even though
5. Because
6. Even though
7. even though
8. because

PRACTICE 8, p. 173

1. even though
2. because
3. Because
4. Even though
5. even though
6. because
7. because
8. even though

PRACTICE 9, p. 174

1. c
2. a
3. b
4. b
5. a
6. c
7. b
8. a

PRACTICE 10, p. 175

1. if it ~~will rain~~ tomorrow — rains
2. If my car doesn't start tomorrow morning — no change
3. If I have any free time during my work day — no change
4. if I ~~will have~~ some free time tomorrow — have
5. If we don't leave within the next ten minutes, we ~~are~~ late — will be
6. If we ~~will leave~~ within the next ten minutes — leave
7. if the population ~~will continue~~ to grow at the present rate — continues

PRACTICE 11, p. 175

1. a. so   b. does
   Meaning: If Tom lives near you
2. a. so   b. are
   Meaning: If you are a resident of Springfield
3. a. not   b. don't
   Meaning: If you don't have enough money
4. a. so   b. are
   Meaning: If you are going to do the laundry
5. a. so   b. did
   Meaning: If I left the water running in the sink

PRACTICE 12, p. 176

1. doesn't approve . . . approves
2. can afford . . . can't afford
3. is raining . . . isn't raining
4. don't understand . . . understand
5. don't want to . . . whether you want to

PRACTICE 13, p. 176

1. unless you can stand the heat
2. unless it is broken
3. unless you cooperate with your opponents

PRACTICE 14. p. 177

1. he wants something
2. she runs out of clean clothes
3. the temperature outside goes below 50 degrees F
4. it is absolutely necessary to get somewhere quickly
5. will you get into Halley College
6. could I afford a big house like that

PRACTICE 15, p. 177

1. pass
2. not going to go
3. rains
4. in case
5. only if
6. always eat
7. even if
8. whether
9. won't
10. don't wake
11. if
12. can we

PRACTICE 16, p. 178

1. h
2. g
3. a
4. f
5. b
6. d
7. e
8. c

PRACTICE 17, p. 178

1. b
2. b
3. d
4. a
5. b
6. c
7. d
8. b
9. c
10. a

CHAPTER 18: REDUCTION OF ADVERB CLAUSES TO MODIFYING ADVERBIAL PHRASES

PRACTICE 1, p. 180

1. While they were riding in the car for six hours
2. While riding in the car for six hours
3. Before taking our long car trip across the country
4. While watching the exciting basketball game on TV
5. While they were watching the exciting basketball game on TV
6. Before leaving for the airport
7. while we were walking on the beach this afternoon
8. while walking on the beach this afternoon
9. While I was trying to get a taxi
10. Before getting into a taxi

PRACTICE 2, p. 180

Grammatically correct items:
2, 3, 4, 6, 8, 10

PRACTICE 3, p. 181

1. ~~he opened~~ — opening
2. ~~I left~~ — leaving
3. ~~I had met~~ — meeting / having met
4. ~~I searched~~ — searching
5. ~~he was herding~~ — herding
6. ~~they marched~~ — marching
7. ~~she was flying~~ — flying
8. ~~they imported~~ — importing

PRACTICE 4, p. 181

1. a. leaving
   b. left
2. a. invented / had invented
   b. inventing / having invented
3. a. working
   b. was working
4. a. flies
   b. flying
5. a. studied
   b. studying
6. a. learning
   b. learned
7. a. taking
   b. take
8. a. was driving
   b. driving

PRACTICE 5, p. 182

Subjects

1. Adv. clause: Sam   Main clause: car   (no change)
2. Adv. clause: Sam   Main clause: he
   While driving to work, Sam had a flat tire.
3. Adv. clause: Nick   Main clause: son   (no change)
4. Adv. clause: Nick   Main clause: he
   Before leaving on his trip, Nick gave his itinerary to his secretary.
5. Adv. clause: Tom   Main clause: he
   After working in the garden all afternoon, Tom took a shower and then . . .
6. Adv. clause: Sunita   Main clause: they   (no change)
7. Adv. clause: a friend   Main clause: American (no change)
8. Adv. clause: she   Main clause: Emily
   Emily always straightens her desk before leaving the office at the end of the day.

PRACTICE 6, p. 183

Modifying Adverbial Phrases

1. Riding his bicycle to school   a
2. Being seven feet tall   b
3. Driving to work this morning   a
4. Running five miles on a very hot day   a, b
5. Having run for 26 miles in the marathon   b
6. Drinking a tall glass of soothing iced tea   a, b
7. Clapping loudly at the end of the game   a
8. Speaking with her guidance counselor   a
9. Knowing that I was going to miss the plane because of heavy traffic   b
10. Having missed my plane   b
11. Waiting for my plane to depart   a

PRACTICE 7, p. 184

1. h
2. i
3. j
4. b
5. d
6. a
7. c
8. f
9. e
10. g

PRACTICE 8, p. 184

1. b, c
2. a, b, c
3. a, b
4. a, b
5. a, c
6. b, c
7. a, c

PRACTICE 9, p. 185

1. a. Upon receiving her acceptance letter for medical school, Sarah
   b. On receiving her acceptance letter for medical school, Sarah
2. a. Upon hearing the sad news,
   b. When she heard the sad news,
3. a. On looking at the accident victim,
   b. When they looked at the accident victim,

PRACTICE 10, p. 185

1. (d) arriving at the airport.
2. (e) reaching the other side of the lake
3. (c) discovering a burnt-out wire
4. (a) learning that the problem was not at all serious
5. (b) being told she got it

PRACTICE 11, p. 186

1. d
2. a
3. f
4. i
5. j
6. h
7. g
8. b
9. e
10. c

CHAPTER 19: CONNECTIVES THAT EXPRESS CAUSE AND EFFECT, CONTRAST, AND CONDITION

PRACTICE 1, p. 187

1. b, c, f
2. a, d, e
3. a, c, e
4. b, d, f

PRACTICE 2, p. 187

1. because
2. because
3. due to / because of
4. because
5. due to / because of
6. because
7. because
8. due to / because of

PRACTICE 3, p. 188

1. heavy traffic
2. there was heavy traffic
3. he is getting old
4. his age
5. she is afraid of heights.
6. her fear of heights
7. a cancellation
8. there was a cancellation today

PRACTICE 4, p. 188

1. . . . headache,
2. No change
3. . . . headache,
4. No change
5. . . . headache. **T**
6. . . . headache. **S**he, therefore, . . .
7. . . . headache. **S**he . . . , therefore.
8. . . . headache, . . .

PRACTICE 5, p. 188

Sentence 1.
1. a
2. b
3. c

Sentence 2.
1. a
2. b
3. a
4. b

PRACTICE 6, p. 189

1. a. I bought lemonade . . . didn't have any orange juice
    b. the store didn't have any orange juice, I bought lemonade
    c. The store didn't have any orange juice. . . . I bought lemonade.
    d. The store didn't have any orange juice. . . . I bought lemonade.
2. a. Mel has excellent grades. Therefore, he will go to a top university.
    b. Mel has excellent grades. He, therefore, will go to a top university.
    c. Mel has excellent grades. He will go to a top university, therefore.
    d. Mel has excellent grades, so he will go to a top university.
3. a. there had been no rain for several months, the crops died.
    b. There had been no rain for several months. . . . the crops died.
    c. There had been no rain for several months. The crops, therefore, died.
    d. There had been no rain for several months, so the crops died.

PRACTICE 7, p. 190

Part I.
1. Because
2. Therefore,
3. because of
4. Therefore,
5. Therefore,
6. because of
7. Because . . . town,
8. Because of

Part II.
9. Due to
10. Since . . . eyesight,
11. . Consequently,
12. . . . heights. Consequently,
13. due to
14. . Consequently,
15. Since

PRACTICE 8, p. 190

1. . . . **Therefore**, . . .
2. No change.
3. . . . **He** simply . . .
4. . . . reservation,
5. . **Therefore**, . . .
6. . . . orders, . . .
7. No change.
8. . . . . **The** button . . . years ago. **The** zipper . . .
9. . . . unique. **N**o two zebras . . .
10. No change.

PRACTICE 9, p. 191

Sentence 1.
a. Because she ate some bad food, Kim got sick.
b. Because of some bad food, Kim got sick.
c. Kim ate some bad food, so she got sick.
d. Due to some bad food, Kim got sick.

Sentence 2.
a. Adam had driven for thirteen hours. Therefore, he was exhausted.
b. Since Adam had driven for thirteen hours, he was exhausted.
c. Due to the fact that Adam had driven for thirteen hours, he was exhausted.
d. Adam had driven for thirteen hours, so he was exhausted.

PRACTICE 10, p. 191

1. such
2. so
3. so
4. such
5. such
6. so
7. so
8. such
9. so
10. so

PRACTICE 11, p. 192

1. It was such a nice day that we took a walk.
2. The weather was so hot that you could fry an egg on the sidewalk.
3. She talked so fast that I couldn't understand her.
4. It was such an expensive car that we couldn't afford it.
5. There were so few people at the meeting that it was canceled.
6. Ted was so worried about the exam that he couldn't fall asleep last night.
7. The tornado struck with such great force that it lifted automobiles off the ground.
8. Joe's handwriting is so illegible that I can't figure out what this sentence says.
9. David has so many girlfriends that he can't remember all of their names.
10. There were so many people at the meeting that there were not enough seats for everyone.

PRACTICE 12, p. 192

Sentences 1, 3, 4, 5, 7, 8 express purpose

PRACTICE 13, p. 193

1. d
2. i
3. a
4. f
5. j
6. c
7. e
8. g
9. h
10. b

PRACTICE 14, p. 193

1. 1   5. 2
2. 1   6. 2
3. 1   7. 1
4. 2   8. 2

PRACTICE 15, p. 193

1. Rachel turned on the TV so that she could watch the news.
2. Alex wrote down the time and date of his appointment so that he wouldn't forget to go.
3. Nancy is taking extra courses every semester so that she can graduate early.
4. Sue lowered the volume on the TV set so that she wouldn't disturb her roommate.
5. Ed took some change from his pocket so that he could buy a newspaper.
6. I turned on the TV so that I could listen to the news while I was making dinner.
7. I turned off the phone so that I wouldn't be interrupted while I was working.
8. It's a good idea for you to learn keyboarding skills so that you'll be able to use your computer more efficiently.
9. Lynn tied a string around her finger so that she wouldn't forget to take her book back to the library.
10. The Parks Department has placed wastebaskets in convenient places in the park so that people won't litter.

PRACTICE 16, p. 194

1. is   6. isn't
2. is   7. is
3. isn't   8. isn't
4. is   9. isn't
5. is   10. is

PRACTICE 17, p. 194

1. a. Even though
   b. Despite
   c. Despite
   d. Despite
   e. Even though
2. a. In spite of
   b. Although
   c. Although
   d. In spite of
   e. In spite of

3. a. Despite
   b. Although
   c. Despite
   d. Although
   e. Despite
4. a. In spite of
   b. Even though
   c. in spite of
   d. even though
   e. in spite of
   f. even though
   g. even though
   h. in spite of

PRACTICE 18, p. 196

1. e   6. i
2. c   7. d
3. b   8. j
4. g   9. h
5. a   10. f

PRACTICE 19, p. 196

1. a. Even though it was night, we could see the road very clearly.
   b. Although it was night, we could see the road very clearly.
   c. It was night, but we could see the road very clearly.
2. a. Despite the fact that Helen has a fear of heights, she enjoys skydiving.
   b. Despite her fear of heights, Helen enjoys skydiving.
   c. Helen has a fear of heights; nevertheless, she enjoys skydiving.
3. a. Though Millie has the flu, she is working at her computer.
   b. Millie has the flu, but she is working at her computer anyway.
   c. Millie has the flu, but she is still working at her computer.

PRACTICE 20, p. 197

Possible answers

1. Red is bright and lively, while gray is a dull color. OR
   While red is bright and lively, gray is a dull color.
2. Jane is insecure and unsure of herself. Her sister, on the other hand, is full of self-confidence.
3. While a rock is heavy, a feather is light. OR
   A rock is heavy, while a feather is light.
4. Some children are unruly. Others, however, are quiet and obedient. OR
   Some children are unruly; others, however, are quiet and obedient. OR
   Some children are unruly. Others are quiet and obedient, however.
5. Language and literature classes are easy and enjoyable for Alex. On the other hand, math and science courses are difficult for him. OR
   Language and literature classes are easy and enjoyable for Alex; on the other hand, math and science courses are difficult for him.
6. Strikes can bring improvements in wages and working conditions; however, strikes can also cause loss of jobs and bankruptcy. OR
   Strikes can bring improvements in wages and working conditions. Strikes can also cause loss of jobs and bankruptcy, however.

PRACTICE 21, p. 197

Modals in the answers may vary.

1. I am going to have to (should / had better / must) call my mother. Otherwise, she'll start worrying about me.
2. The bus had better come soon. Otherwise, we'll be late for work.
3. You should make a reservation. Otherwise, you won't get seated at the restaurant.
4. Beth should stop complaining. Otherwise, she will lose the few friends she has.
5. You have to have a government-issued ID. Otherwise, you can't get on the plane.
6. Louis has to apply for his driver's license in person. Otherwise, he can't replace it.
7. You have to be a registered voter. Otherwise, you can't vote in the general election.
8. You should clean up the kitchen tonight. Otherwise, you'll have to clean it up early tomorrow.

PRACTICE 22, p. 198

1. e
2. h
3. d
4. g, h
5. b
6. f
7. a
8. c

PRACTICE 23, p. 198

1. exports
2. doesn't export
3. uses
4. is
5. originated
6. is

PRACTICE 24, p. 198

1. passes
2. doesn't pass
3. passes
4. passes
5. doesn't pass
6. passes
7. doesn't pass

PRACTICE 25, p. 199

1. the flowers bloomed
2. I took good care of the garden
3. my care
4. my care
5. , the flowers didn't bloom
6. . . . ; therefore, the flowers didn't bloom
7. ; however, the flowers bloomed
8. . . . garden. **N**evertheless, the flowers did not bloom
9. . . . garden, so the flowers did not bloom
10. . . . garden, the flowers bloomed
11. . . . garden, the flowers didn't bloom
12. the flowers bloomed anyway
13. . . . garden, the flowers will bloom
14. . . . garden, the flowers will not bloom
15. . . . garden. **O**therwise, the flowers will not bloom
16. . . . garden. **C**onsequently, the flowers did not bloom
17. . . . garden. **N**onetheless, the flowers bloomed
18. the flowers will bloom
19. will the flowers bloom
20. , yet the flowers did not bloom
21. the flowers won't bloom
22. or not you take good care of the garden

CHAPTER 20: CONDITIONAL SENTENCES AND WISHES

PRACTICE 1, p. 200

1. a. yes	4. a. no
b. no	b. no
2. a. yes	c. yes
b. no	5. a. no
3. a. no	b. no
b. yes	c. yes
	d. no

PRACTICE 2, p. 200

Group 1
1. c
2. a
3. b

Group 2
1. c
2. a
3. b

Group 3
1. c
2. b
3. a

Group 4
1. a
2. c
3. b

PRACTICE 3, p. 201

1. heat . . . boils
   heat . . . will boil
2. forget . . . look
   forget . . . will look
3. pet . . . purrs
   pet . . . will purr
4. have . . . will call
   have . . . call
5. eat . . . will get
   eat . . . get
6. is . . . are
   is . . . will be

PRACTICE 4, p. 202

1. b
2. a
3. b
4. a
5. b
6. b

PRACTICE 5, p. 202

1. were . . . would be
2. had . . . would travel
3. had . . . would like
4. liked . . . would cook
5. weren't . . . could have
6. didn't have . . . would go / 'd go

PRACTICE 6, p. 203

1. h
2. d
3. b
4. j
5. i
6. c
7. a
8. e
9. g
10. f

PRACTICE 7, p. 203

1. b
2. a
3. a
4. a
5. b
6. b

PRACTICE 8, p. 204

1. had not taken . . . would not have met
2. had not forgotten . . . could have paid
3. had known . . . would have visited
4. had paid . . . would not have cut off
5. had been . . . would not have been canceled
6. had not discovered . . . would not have developed

PRACTICE 9, p. 204

1. c
2. a
3. b
4. e
5. f
6. d

PRACTICE 10, p. 205

1. had . . . could fly
2. could fly . . . would arrive
3. get . . . will have / 'll have
4. have . . . will tell / 'll tell
5. had had . . . would have told him
6. had told . . . would not have been

PRACTICE 11, p. 205

1. If I hadn't been sick yesterday, I would have gone to class.
2. If Alan ate breakfast, he wouldn't overeat at lunch.
3. If his watch had not been slow, Kostas would not have been late to his own wedding.
4. If the bus were not always so crowded, I would ride it to work every morning.
5. If Sara had known that Highway 57 was closed, she would have taken an alternative route.
6. If someone had been there to help her, Camille could have finished unloading the truck.

PRACTICE 12, p. 206

1. If the wind weren't blowing so hard, we could go sailing.
2. If the wind had not been blowing so hard, we could have gone sailing.
3. If the water weren't running, I could hear you.
4. If the water had not been running, I could have heard the phone.
5. If the baby were not hungry, she wouldn't be crying.
6. If Dick had not been sleeping soundly, he would have heard his alarm clock.
7. If I had not been watching an exciting mystery on TV, I would have answered the phone.
8. If I weren't trying to concentrate, I could talk to you now.

PRACTICE 13, p. 206

1. a, c
2. b, d
3. a, d
4. b, c
5. a, d
6. a, d

PRACTICE 14, p. 207

1. If it weren't raining, we would finish the game.
2. If I had eaten lunch, I wouldn't be hungry now.
3. If Bob hadn't left his wallet at home, he would have money for lunch now.
4. If Bruce were not always daydreaming, he would get his work done.
5. If I hadn't played basketball for three hours last night, my muscles wouldn't hurt today.
6. If the band had not been playing so loud, I could have heard what you said.
7. If Diane had not asked the technician a lot of questions, she wouldn't understand how to use her computer now.
8. If Olga and Ivan had been paying attention, they would have seen the exit sign on the highway.
9. If the doctor had explained the test results to me, I would know what they mean.
10. If we had not been sleeping last night, we would have heard the thunder and lightning.

PRACTICE 15, p. 208

1. Were I
2. Should you need
3. Had I known
4. Had I been offered
5. Should anyone call
6. Should the pizza need reheating
7. Should you feel
8. Were you really a lawyer

PRACTICE 16, p. 208

1. c
2. b
3. c
4. b

PRACTICE 17, p. 209

1. I hadn't forgotten to tell him that she needed a ride.
2. you hadn't helped
3. I had opened the door quickly
4. he could have gotten time off from work
5. he had told his boss about the problem

PRACTICE 18, p. 209

1. d
2. a
3. c
4. d
5. c
6. d
7. c
8. b
9. d
10. a
11. c
12. d
13. b
14. d
15. c
16. b
17. b
18. b
19. a
20. c

PRACTICE 19, p. 211

1. b
2. b
3. a
4. b
5. b
6. b

PRACTICE 20, p. 211

1. were shining
2. had gone
3. had driven
4. could swim
5. had won
6. had gotten
7. hadn't quit
8. were winter
9. would sing

PRACTICE 21, p. 212

1. had gone . . . could paint
2. hadn't moved . . . had taken
3. would stop
4. hadn't invited
5. hadn't paid
6. A. . . . would hurry . . .
   B. . . . would relax
7. A. . . . hadn't been elected
   B. . . . hadn't voted
8. A. . . . weren't . . . were
   B. . . . were . . . . were
9. had told
10. would go

PRACTICE 22, p. 213

1. would get
2. would snow
3. would leave
4. would hang up
5. would end
6. would order

PRACTICE 23, p. 213

1. would look
2. had had
3. hadn't been driving
4. would not have slid
5. steps
6. had known

7. would not have crashed
8. had not taken
9. would not have lost
10. had not lost
11. would have had
12. had had
13. would not have to pay
14. hadn't been driving
15. would not have run into
16. would not be
17. were
18. would take
19. stay
20. would stay
21. were not
22. could go
23. will fly
24. will take
25. could drive
26. would be
27. had

APPENDIX: SUPPLEMENTARY GRAMMAR UNITS

PRACTICE 1, p. A1

      S   **V**   **O**
1. Airplanes have wings.

         S   **V**   **O**
2. The teacher explained the problem.

         S   **V**   **O**
3. Children enjoy games.

     S   **V**   **O**
4. Jack wore a blue suit.

         S **V** **O**   **S** **V**
5. Some animals eat plants. Some animals eat
       O
other animals.

                               S
6. According to an experienced waitress, you
     V   **O**
can carry full cups of coffee without spilling

them just by never looking at them.

PRACTICE 2, p. A1

    VI
1. Alice arrived at six o'clock.

    VT
2. We drank some tea.

  VI
3. I agree with you.

   VI
4. I waited for Sam at the airport for two hours.

       VI
5. They're staying at a resort hotel in San Antonio, Texas.

         VT
6. Mr. Chan is studying English.

7. The wind **VI** is blowing hard today.

8. I **VI** walked to the theater, but Janice **VT** rode her bicycle.

9. Crocodiles **VI** hatch from eggs.

10. Rivers **VI** flow toward the sea.

PRACTICE 3, p. A2

1. Jack opened the **ADJ** heavy door **ADV** slowly.

2. **ADJ** Chinese jewelers carved **ADJ** beautiful ornaments from jade.

3. The **ADJ** old man carves **ADJ** wooden figures **ADV** skillfully.

4. A **ADJ** busy executive **ADV** usually has **ADJ** short conversations on the telephone.

5. The **ADJ** young woman had a **ADV** very **ADJ** good time at the picnic **ADV** yesterday.

PRACTICE 4, p. A2

1. quickly	8. usually
2. quick	9. well
3. polite	10. good
4. politely	11. gentle
5. regularly	12. gently
6. regular	13. bad
7. usual	14. badly

PRACTICE 5, p. A3

1. Sue **always takes** a walk in the morning.
2. Tim **is always** a hard worker.
3. Beth **has always worked** hard.
4. Jack **always works** hard.
5. **Do you always work** hard?
6. Taxis **are usually** available . . . .
7. Yusef **rarely takes** a taxi . . . .
8. I **have often thought** about . . . .
9. Yuko **probably needs** some help.
10. **Have you ever attended** the show . . . ?
11. Al **seldom goes** out . . . .
12. The students **are hardly ever** late.
13. **Do you usually finish** your . . . ?
14. In India, the monsoon season **generally begins** . . .
15. . . . Mr. Singh's hometown **usually receives** around . . . .

PRACTICE 6, p. A3

1. Jim came to class <u>without</u> his books.
2. We stayed <u>at</u> home <u>during</u> the storm.
3. Sonya walked <u>across</u> the bridge <u>over</u> the Cedar River.
4. When Alex walked <u>through</u> the door, his little sister ran <u>toward</u> him and put her arms <u>around</u> his neck.
5. The two <u>of</u> us need to talk <u>to</u> Tom too.
6. Animals live <u>in</u> all parts <u>of</u> the world. Animals walk or crawl <u>on</u> land, fly <u>in</u> the air, and swim <u>in</u> the water.
7. Scientists divide living things <u>into</u> two main groups: the animal kingdom and the plant kingdom.
8. Asia extends <u>from</u> the Pacific Ocean <u>in</u> the east <u>to</u> Africa and Europe <u>in</u> the west.

PRACTICE 7, p. A4

1. **S** Jack **V** put the **O** letter **PP** in the mailbox.

2. The **S** children **V** walked **PP** to school.

3. **S** Mary **V** did her **O** homework **PP** at the library.

4. Chinese **S** printers **V** created the first paper **O** money **PP** in the world.

5. Dark **S** clouds **V** appeared **PP** on the horizon.

6. **S** Mary **V** filled the **O** shelves **PP** of the cabinet **PP** with boxes **PP** of old books.

PRACTICE 8, p. A4

	L.VERB +	**ADJ**
1.	Ø (no linking verb in the sentence)	
2.	looked	fresh
3.	Ø	
4.	Ø	
5.	tasted	good
6.	grew	quiet
7.	Ø	
8.	Ø	
9.	Ø	
10.	smells	delicious
11.	Ø	
12.	got	sleepy
13.	became	rough
14.	Ø	
15.	Ø	
16.	sounded	happy
17.	turns	hot
18.	Ø	
19.	Ø	
20.	appears	certain
21.	seems	strange

PRACTICE 9, p. A5

1. clean	9. well
2. slowly	10. fair
3. safely	11. terrible
4. anxious	12. good
5. complete	13. light
6. wildly	14. confidently
7. honest	15. famous
8. thoughtfully	16. fine

PRACTICE 10, p. A6

	Question word	Auxiliary verb	Subject	Main verb	Rest of question
1a.	Ø	Can	Bob	live	there?
1b.	Where	can	Bob	live	Ø?
1c.	Who	can	Ø	live	there?
2a.	Ø	**Is**	**Ron**	**living**	there?
2b.	Where	**is**	**Ron**	**living**	Ø?
2c.	Who	**is**	Ø	**living**	there?
3a.	Ø	**Does**	**Sue**	**live**	there?
3b.	Where	**does**	**Sue**	**live**	Ø?
3c.	Who	Ø	Ø	**lives**	there?
4a.	Ø	**Will**	**Ann**	**live**	there?
4b.	Where	**will**	**Ann**	**live**	Ø?
4c.	Who	**will**	Ø	**live**	there?
5a.	Ø	**Did**	**Jack**	**live**	there?
5b.	**Where**	**did**	**Jack**	**live**	Ø?
5c.	**Who**	Ø	Ø	**lived**	there?
6a.	Ø	**Has**	**Mary**	**lived**	**there?**
6b.	**Where**	**has**	**Mary**	**lived**	Ø?
6c.	**Who**	**has**	Ø	**lived**	**there?**

PRACTICE 11, p. A7

1. When are you going to the zoo?
2. Are you going downtown later today?
3. Do you live in an apartment?
4. Where does Sue live?
5. Who lives in that house?
6. Can you speak French?
7. Who can speak Arabic?
8. When did Olga arrive?
9. Who arrived late?
10. What is Ann opening?
11. What is Ann doing?
12. What did Mary open?
13. Who opened the door?
14. Has the mail arrived?
15. Do you have a bicycle?
16. What does Alex have in his hand?
17. Do you like ice cream?
18. Would you like an ice cream cone?
19. What would Joe like?
20. Who would like a soft drink?

PRACTICE 12, p. A8

1. How do you take your coffee?
2. What kind of dictionary do you have? (have you? / have you got?)
3. What does he do for a living?
4. Who was Margaret talking to? / To whom was Margaret talking?
5. How many people showed up for the meeting?
6. Why could none of the planes take off?
7. What was she thinking about? / About what was she thinking?
8. How fast / How many miles per hour (OR: an hour) were you driving when the police officer stopped you?
9. What kind of food do you like best?
10. Which apartment is yours?
11. What is Oscar like? (*also possible:* What kind of person / man is Oscar?)
12. What does Oscar look like?
13. Whose dictionary fell to the floor?
14. Why isn't Abby here?
15. When will all of the students in the class be informed of their final grades?
16. How do you feel?
17. Which book did you prefer?
18. What kind of music do you like?
19. How late is the plane expected to be?
20. Why did the driver of the stalled car light a flare?
21. Which pen do you want?
22. What's the weather like in July?
23. How do you like your steak?
24. How did you do on the test?
25. How many seconds are there in a year?

PRACTICE 13, p. A9

1. How much money do you need?
2. Where was Roberto born? / In what country/city was . . .? / What country/city was Roberto born in?
3. How often do you go out to eat?
4. Who(m) are you waiting for? (*very formal and seldom used:* For whom are you waiting?)
5. Who answered the phone?
6. Who(m) did you call?
7. Who called?
8. How much gas/How many gallons of gas did she buy?
9. What does *deceitful* mean?
10. What is an abyss?
11. Which way did he go?
12. Whose books and papers are these?
13. How many children do they have? [*British or regional American:* How many children have they?]
14. How long has he been here?
15. How far is it / How many miles is it to Madrid?
16. When / At what time can the doctor see me?
17. Who **is** her roommate?
18. Who **are** her roommates?
19. How long / How many years have your parents been living there?
20. Whose book is this?
21. Who's coming over for dinner?
22. What color **is** Ann's dress?
23. What color **are** Ann's eyes?
24. Who can't go . . . ?
25. Why **can't Bob** go? / How come **Bob can't** go?

26. Why **didn't you** / How come **you didn't** answer . . . ? *(formal and rare:* Why **did you not** answer the phone?)
27. What kind of music do you like?
28. What don't you understand?
29. What **is** Janet **doing** right now?
30. How do you spell *sitting*? [*you* = impersonal pronoun]
31. What **does** Tom **look like**?
32. What **is** Tom **like**?
33. What does Ron do (for a living)?
34. How far / How many miles is Mexico from here?
35. How do you take / like your coffee?
36. Which (city) is farther north, Stockholm or Moscow? / Of Stockholm and Moscow, which (city/one) is farther north?
37. How are you getting along?

PRACTICE 14, p. A10
1. Haven't you seen . . . ? No.
2. Don't you feel . . . ? No.
3. Wasn't he . . . ? No.
4. Didn't Mary tell . . . ? No.
5. Don't Janet and you work . . . ? Yes.
6. Isn't that . . . ? Yes.
7. Wasn't she . . . ? No.
8. Isn't she . . . ? Yes.

PRACTICE 15, p. A11
1. don't you
2. have you
3. didn't she
4. aren't there
5. have you
6. don't you *(also possible but less common:* haven't you)
7. won't you
8. doesn't he
9. shouldn't we
10. can they
11. are they
12. isn't it
13. didn't they
14. aren't I
15. isn't it

PRACTICE 16, p. A11
1. He's
2. Ø
3. He's
4. Ø
5. She'd
6. Ø
7. She'd
8. Ø
9. We'll
10. They're
11. It's
12. It's
13. Ø
14. Ø
15. We're
16. Ø

17. She's
18. She'd
19. She'd . . . we'd
20. Ø . . . he'd

PRACTICE 17, p. A12
1. I don't have any problems. I have no problems.
2. There wasn't any food on the shelf. There was no food on the shelf.
3. I didn't receive any letters from home. I received no letters from home.
4. I don't need any help. I need no help.
5. We don't have any time to waste. We have no time to waste.
6. You shouldn't have given the beggar any money. You should have given the beggar no money.
7. I don't trust anyone. I trust no one.
8. I didn't see anyone. I saw no one.
9. There wasn't anyone in his room. There was no one in his room.
10. She can't find anybody who knows about it. She can find nobody who knows about it.

PRACTICE 18, p. A13
1. We **have no** time to waste. OR We **don't have any** time to waste.
2. I **didn't have any** problems. OR I **had no** problems.
3. I **can't do anything** about it. OR I **can do nothing** about it.
4. You **can hardly ever understand** her when she speaks.
5. I **know neither** Ann **nor** her husband. OR I **don't know either** Ann **or** her husband.
6. **Don't ever drink** water from . . . . OR **Never drink** water from . . . .
7. . . . I **could barely hear** the speaker.

PRACTICE 19, p. A13
1. **Hardly had I stepped** out of bed . . . .
2. **Never will I say** that again.
3. **Scarcely ever have I enjoyed** myself more . . . .
4. **Rarely does she make** a mistake.
5. **Never will I trust** him again because . . . .
6. **Hardly ever is it** possible to get . . . .
7. **Seldom do I skip** breakfast.
8. **Never have I known** a more . . . .

PRACTICE 20, p. A13
1. honesty, fairness
2. school, class
3. her illness, her husband's death
4. jail, prison
5. ghosts, UFOs
6. my cousin, a friend
7. mathematics, sports
8. you, your children
9. smoking, cigarettes
10. magazines, a newspaper, websites

PRACTICE 21, p. A14

1. of
2. at
3. from
4. in
5. at
6. of
7. to
8. for
9. on
10. from

PRACTICE 22, p. A14

Situation 1:

1. to
2. to
3. of
4. to
5. with
6. to
7. to

Situation 2:

1. with/by
2. with
3. with
4. of
5. of
6. of, by

PRACTICE 23, p. A15

1. c
2. e
3. b
4. f
5. a
6. g
7. d

PRACTICE 24, p. A15

1. to
2. for
3. from
4. on
5. about
6. for
7. about
8. with
9. on
10. with
11. on
12. of

PRACTICE 25, p. A16

1. for
2. for
3. of
4. to . . . for
5. with
6. to
7. on
8. for . . . to
9. about
10. of
11. of
12. to / with
13. with
14. to

PRACTICE 26, p. A16

Sample answers:

1. be
2. arrive
3. tell
4. talk
5. write
6. see
7. become
8. be

PRACTICE 27, p. A17

1. take
2. be named
3. stay
4. be postponed
5. be admitted
6. be controlled . . . (be) eliminated
7. have
8. be
9. know
10. be
11. be permitted
12. not be
13. return
14. be built
15. not tell
16. be told

PRACTICE 28, p. A18

1. raised
2. rises
3. sat
4. set
5. lay
6. lying
7. laid
8. lie
9. lies
10. raises
11. rose
12. lays
13. laid
14. set
15. sat
16. lies

SPECIAL WORKBOOK SECTION: PHRASAL VERBS

PRACTICE 1, p. A21

1. a. after
   b. over
   c. up
   d. into
2. a. out
   b. into
   c. out
   d. out of
3. a. over
   b. through with
   c. out of
   d. back from
   e. off
4. a. off
   b. up
   c. on
   d. back
   e. in

PRACTICE 2, p. A22

1. passed out
2. Pick out
3. takes after
4. think . . . over
5. puts up with
6. passed away
7. show up
8. get along with
9. turn in
10. pass out

PRACTICE 3, p. A23

1. our assignment?
2. a lie. / a story.
3. the city. / the banks.
4. your cigarette. / the lights. / the fire.
5. the war? / the crisis?
6. the problem? / the puzzle?
7. the lights? / the music? / the printer?
8. his classmate. / a girl.
9. chocolate. / smoking.
10. a friend. / a classmate.
11. high school. / college.

PRACTICE 4, p. A23

1. into
2. off
3. on
4. back
5. out
6. up
7. into . . . out
8. up
9. up
10. on

PRACTICE 5, p. A24
1. away / out
2. up
3. off / out
4. up
5. off
6. up
7. about, on
8. out of
9. off
10. off . . . in

PRACTICE 6, p. A25
1. out
2. back
3. by / in
4. on . . . off
5. put . . . out
6. up
7. up . . . away / out
8. out . . . back
9. up
10. on

PRACTICE 7, p. A27
1. up
2. over
3. after
4. up
5. out
6. down
7. up
8. out
9. off
10. up
11. out

PRACTICE 8, p. A28
1. back
2. up
3. out
4. over
5. on . . . off
6. in . . . out
7. on . . . off
8. on . . . off
9. up with
10. A: about / on
    B: along with
11. A: over . . . in
    B: over

NOTES